Healing Healthcare

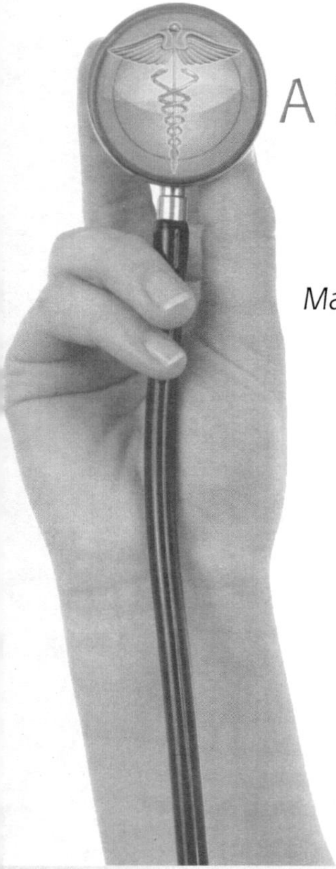

A Leadership Journey

Mark L. Dean PhD

GOAL/QPC

Healing Healthcare,
A Leadership Journey

Mark L. Dean PhD, *Author*
Bob King, *Foreword*
Larry Smith, *Editor*
Janet MacCausland, *Graphic Design*
Susan Griebel, *Project Manager*

GOAL/QPC

8E Industrial Way, Suite 3, Salem, NH 03079

800.643.4316 or 603.890.8800

service@goalqpc.com

goalqpc.com or MemoryJogger.org

Printed in the United States of America

First Edition 10 9 8 7 6 5 4 3 2

ISBN 978-1-57861-140-5

Acknowledgments

Much like the transformation of a healthcare system, the successful development and publication of a book is truly a team effort. The author plays the lead role, but without the able assistance of many others it will not be a success. My sincere thanks go out to the people who reviewed the draft version of this book. Their thoughtful suggestions improved the work immeasurably, and their words of encouragement helped bring it to fruition. I am also indebted to the great team at GOAL/QPC—Bob, Sue, Dan, and Janet—without whose patient and able assistance this book would not be.

Special thanks to Jenny Dean who labored long and hard to put a more humanistic touch on the book. Without her contributions the book may have read more like what it was: something written by an engineer. A special note of thanks to my wife, Bev Dean. Without her continuing support and encouragement the book would not have been completed.

Thomas Gessel, *Chief Executive Officer*
Saints Mary & Elizabeth Hospital

John Dean, *Business Improvement Coordinator*
First Quantum Minerals

Mike Mudd, *Lean Improvement Expert*
Jewish Hospital & St. Mary's HealthCare

Janice James, *Managing Partner*
HuronHealthcare

David Graffy, *Chief Executive Officer*
ProLift Equipment

Jennifer Dean, *Patient Care*
Advanced Endodontics

Marty Bonick, *Vice President Operations,*
Community Health Systems

Timothy Jarm, *President*/CEO
Alliant Management Services

Robert Strickland, *Senior Vice President*
Catholic Health Initiatives, Inc.

Publisher's Foreword

Quality consultants often complain about silos in organizations, but then proceed to create silos in quality. Each consultant takes the same tools and puts a different name on it resulting in the impression of "flavor of the month". How refreshing it is to publish this book which integrates many different important elements into a seamless masterpiece.

For my part I have grown to see the different approaches that have evolved over the last thirty years as a quality Hierarchy. And I give credit to Bertrand Jouslin de Noray of France for suggesting the transformation and getting to the essential levels.

The hierarchy is modeled after Maslow's hierarchy. There is often a progression from the lower level which is more basic to the higher levels that are more difficult and advanced. Each level builds on the lower levels.

- At the basic level is inspection and quality audits. It performs the important role of determining what is conforming and what is not.

- The second level is total quality management. The organization builds on the basic level and engages all employees in improvement with the managers working on the system and the employees giving insight because they are closer to what is really going on.

- The third level is lean six sigma. This builds on the two lower levels by focusing on a company-wide improvement plan and ties each improvement project to that plan. It also adds statistical tools and lean tools that improve the effectiveness of the improvement effort.

- The fourth level is creativity and innovation. This level corrects the number one weakness of the lower levels by supplying tools to generate new ideas at the beginning, intermediate and advanced level. These tools are selected based on the level of difficulty of the problems and the level of sophistication of those on the team.

- The fifth level is the transformation and organizational breakthrough level. This level ties together the goals of the organization with the goals of individual employees. It adds the best of organizational development and good change theory and practice.

- The sixth level corresponds to Maslow's self-actualization level. It looks to the purpose of the organization and looks to issues such as sustainability, spirituality and improving the planet.

In his short but powerful book, Dr. Mark Dean coaches us as he relates a story of one CEO mentoring another CEO and each CEO coaching their reports in ways that assure ultimate success. Dr. Dean integrates artfully different levels of the hierarchy with a primary focus on lean and transformation, thus helping health care executives break down the myths of flavor of the month.

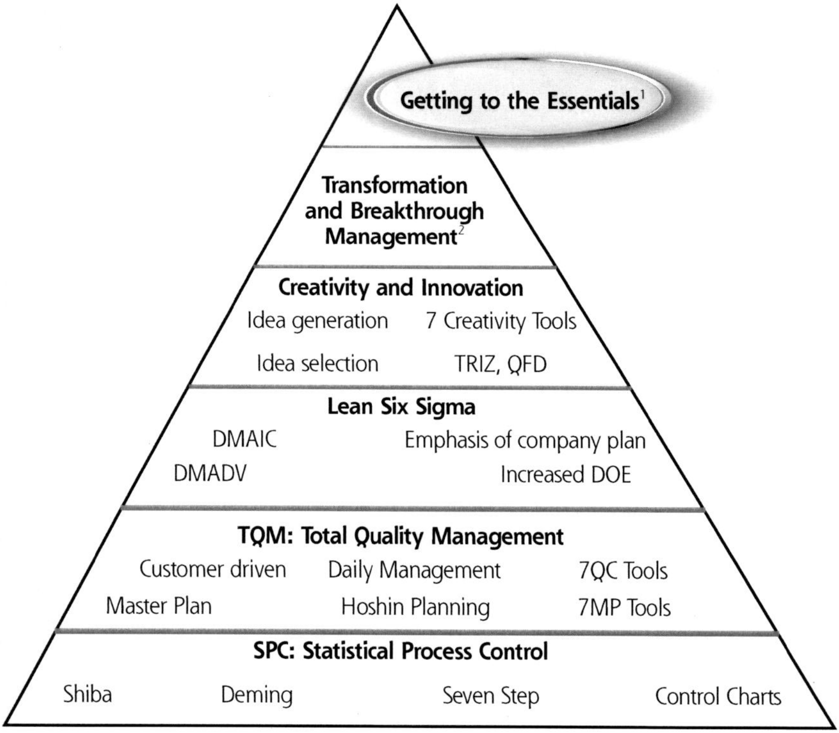

Although some may be surprised by the use of the word transformation, it has a long history predating the rise of quality in the last thirty years. To some, it will be better remembered as organizational design and organizational development.

The diagram on the next page shows the relationship between the continuous improvement of products and processes and the continuous improvement of standards.

1) Getting to the Essentials. Preserving the company while preserving the planet.
2) Transformation & Breakthrough Management. Alignment of individual and company visions.

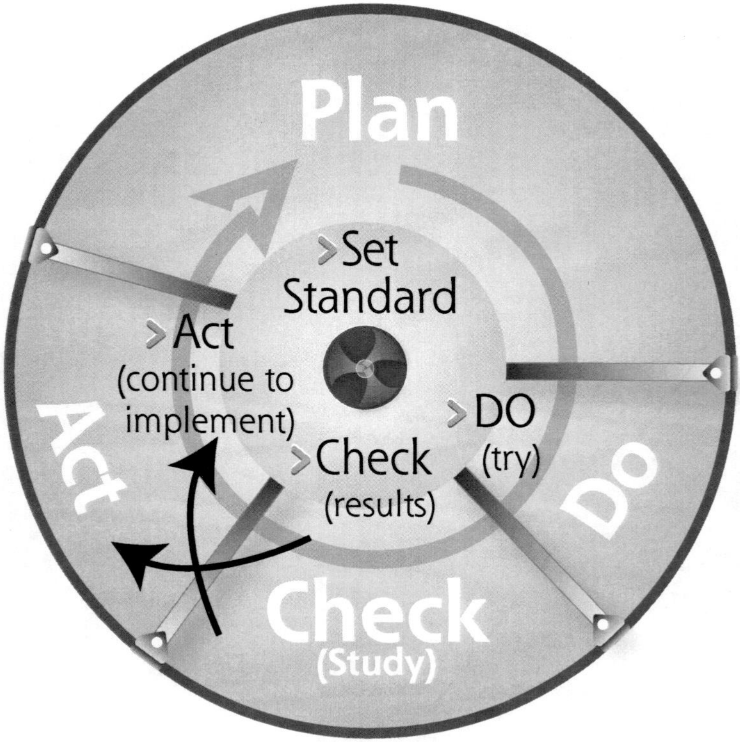

The process begins with continuous improvement. If the check (study) step shows success with new approach then shift into standardize cycle set and implement standards. If the check (study) step of the standards cycle shows a problem, there is a shift to continuous improvement cycle until an improvement is proven.

Hope you enjoy this treatise. And as always we at GOAL/QPC look forward to your feedback and suggestions for future books.

Bob King
CEO and founder GOAL/QPC
bobking@goalqpc.com

This story is fictitious.

But if you join Will Patterson and Healing University on their journey, it could become your journey.

Destination: Perfect Care

Table of Contents

Introduction

I'm Will Patterson, CEO of Healing University Medical Center, and this is our story. When I started this job about three and a half years ago, I could not have even begun to imagine the journey on which I had embarked. I took the job because I wanted a challenge, and turning around Healing University Medical Center was going to be just that. At the beginning, the task at times seemed overwhelming. Over time, there were rewards beyond my wildest imagination. In between, there was a lot of hard work, perseverance, and many lessons to be learned. This story is about our transformation.

Our transformation would not have been possible without the advice and unwavering support of a wise and seasoned CEO, Paul Sage. Paul served as a teacher, mentor and sounding board. He introduced me to Lean, an approach to process improvement that he had successfully applied in his system, Mercy Medical. Over the course of time I discovered that Lean fosters not only process improvement but, equally important, cultural transformation.

Lean focuses on improving the flow of patients through the system while also enhancing their care. It achieves these ends by empowering team members to objectively evaluate and improve their work processes. This simple but powerful act of empowerment has the added benefit of stimulating a cultural transformation from the bottom up. Thus, Lean and cultural transformations are two sides of the same coin. The act of empowering team members to improve their processes enables both the cultural transformation and process improvement.

One of the great learnings I had along the way was the concept of Healing Pathways. Lean was initially developed to improve the flow of 'things,' like widgets and information, through a series of processes that together comprise what is called a Value Stream. It understandably neglects the perspective and perceptions of the widgets and information that flow through these Value Streams. We realized that a different approach was needed in health care. In health care, the most important things in our Value Streams are people, not inanimate objects. When improving processes through which patients flow, we must also consider the impact on the patients, from their perspective. We began to call these types of processes Healing Pathways—value streams through which patients flow—and we developed analyses and tools to evaluate such Pathways from the patients' perspective.

I learned a lot along the way. I am a much stronger and wiser leader for the struggle.

- Leadership is the key. What leaders should do is empower their people to improve processes to achieve excellent organizational performance.

- It's about the people and the process – together they provide patient care. It is truly through well-developed and empowered people that the best processes in support of patient care are developed and implemented.

- Management owns the system, and is responsible for ensuring that the system works *for* the people; not against them. It is management's job to eliminate barriers to success, allowing our people to be the best and most effective they can be.

- Lean is not magic. It's a tool that, in the hands of motivated and persevering leaders, can be a key to organizational transformation. Consultants, the performance improvement group, and Black Belts can facilitate events, provide education on Lean concepts and their application, and provide recommendations for process improvement. But it is only the process owners—i.e., the leaders of the organization—that can actually initiate, implement, and hold the gains. The leaders—management—owns the system, and they are responsible for its improvement.

- Much like fertilizer in the hands of an able gardener, Lean can nurture the tree of organizational excellence, and its mighty boughs of cultural transformation and process improvement; helping it reach upwards towards the heavens – drawing ever closer and yet never quite reaching perfection. In the context of process flow, and highly motivated and satisfied team members and physicians, Lean can also be the Way to excellent patient care—the Healing Way.

— Will Patterson, CEO
Healing University Medical Center

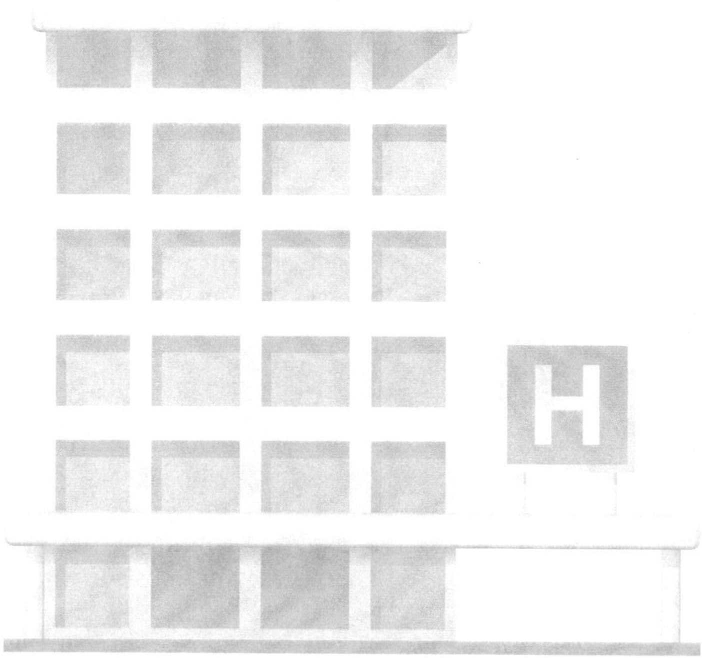

Chapter ONE

What Have I Gotten Myself Into?

This adventure started just over three years ago. I was about a month into my new role as CEO of Healing University Medical Center. We are a medium-sized system, including Healing University Hospital, an academic medical center and the region's Level I trauma center, and two ambulatory care centers—Medical Center East and Medical Center North—at which we provide emergency care, imaging, and outpatient surgery.

It had been a long day, like the many long days I'd had since taking over. I'd just gotten done meeting with Dr. Jackson. He was upset with us because his patient was forty-five minutes late getting to the OR. And that was the second time this week that we didn't have his patient ready for him. I couldn't blame him. I knew we had some issues there. But our ED was backed up to the point that we were on diversion—mainly because of patients waiting for beds. I'd been trying to get that logjam busted loose for the last couple hours. The sad thing was that I knew we had open beds. But the process of getting patients there just wasn't humming. In fact, it was hardly working at all.

Our Patient Satisfaction scores were in the tank, with below average top-box scores in all three of our hospitals (*see next page*).

I knew that if we were measuring it, our physician satisfaction scores wouldn't have been any better. Healing U (that's what we call it) is old; and it's tough to get great patient satisfaction scores without a shiny new building. But as I sat there rubbing my temples, I had to be honest with myself. That's not the only reason our scores were low. We didn't get to call lights quickly enough, environmental services was stretched too thin to really do a good job; and the truth was our nursing staff was just not as patient focused as they needed to be. They were good people, but they were just plain worn out—working

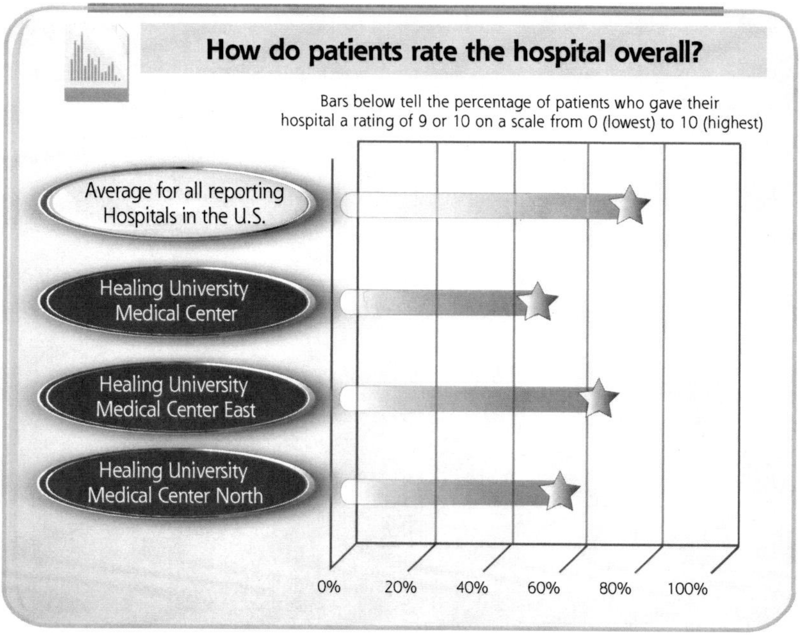

fifty to sixty hours a week, week in, week out. With our high rate of no-shows, and nursing turnover at over eighteen percent, it was all we could do to keep our beds staffed at all.

That led to the next honest question I had to ask myself: Why did we have such high nursing turnover? Well, since they were working so many hours a week, and since there was such a high rate of no-shows, people got frustrated, worn out, and found other jobs. But that was because we couldn't retain adequate staffing levels. And we couldn't retain adequate staffing levels because we had such high turnover rate. . . What a vicious cycle!

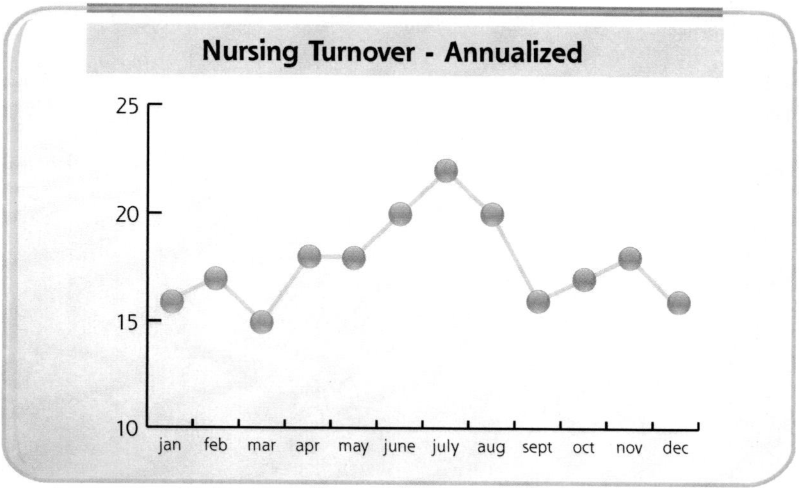

"But look on the bright side," I thought to myself, trying to find something encouraging. We do provide pretty good patient care. Not that our core measure results demonstrated that, but we had some pretty dilapidated IT systems and if you don't document that you did something, well, it just didn't happen. For example, I knew we were giving patients discharge instructions, but we just didn't document it well. Our care is good; we just don't have any evidence to support it.

And that's what I believed.

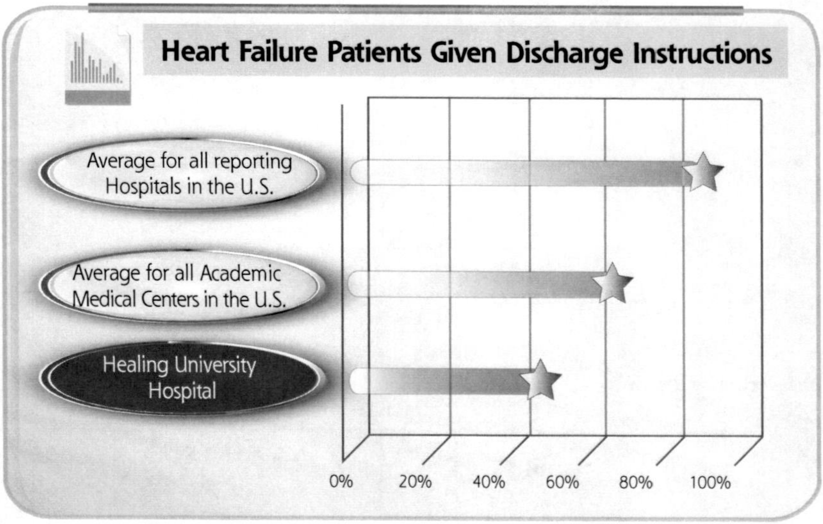

To add to our challenges, one of our local competitors had just opened an ambulatory care center and in so doing got 23 percent of our outpatient surgery volume, and a similar share of our imaging. The docs continued to remind me - in no uncertain terms - that *their* surgeries started on time, *their* nurses were friendly and professional, *their* supplies were there when they needed them, and *their* patients had an overall great experience with sat scores above the 90th percentile. But I couldn't do much about that. We were strapped for capital. After losing money the last four years in a row, we were lucky to be able to replace the magnetron on our MRI that kept shocking people, much less make other less than mandatory improvements. And it was not just about capital—we were just plain strapped for cash. We were sitting at days A/R in the 65 range, with less than 100 days cash on hand. I was just four short weeks into this new job and already the board was breathing down my neck looking for improvement in our operational results.

And like every other health care provider, we faced increased challenges with reduced payments, increased bad debts, and further Medicare cuts looming.

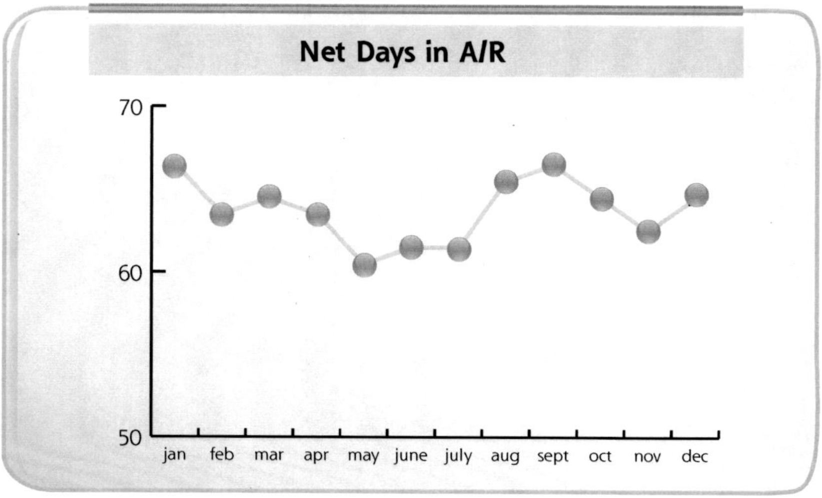

Consequently, we had lost money in each of the last four years, and it was getting worse and not better.

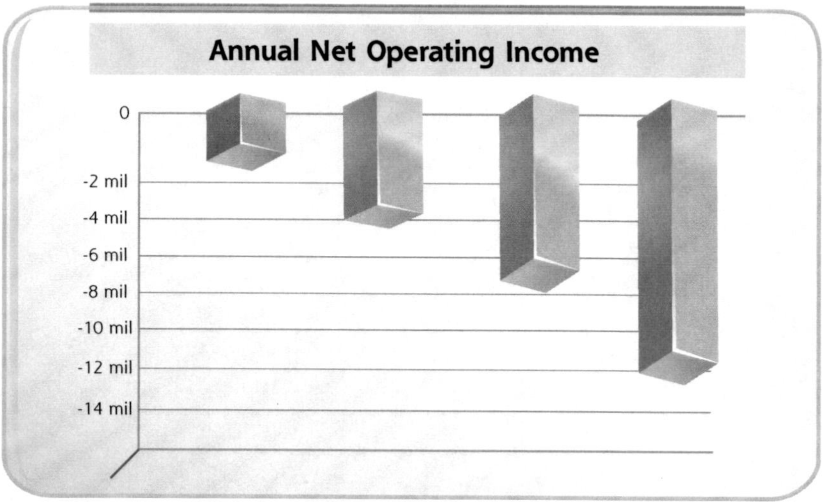

Market share was also declining. It had eroded from 44 percent to just 38 percent in the last three years.

In the past I had always enjoyed the challenge of starting at a new hospital and molding it to what I wanted it to be. During my interview process at Healing U I was informed of the severe decline in the net operating revenue and our current market share position. I'm a num-

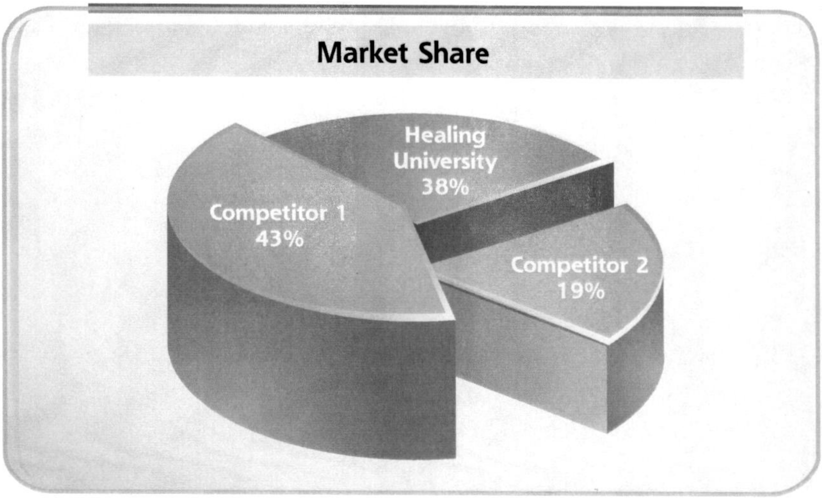

bers guy, and showing me that kind of data really gets my attention. I was intrigued by the challenge of turning Healing U around.

During the interview process I also got anecdotal information that our patient care wasn't at all what it needed to be. My wife Amy is an RN, and has a passion for working with the frail and elderly in nursing home settings. So while I was interviewing for the Healing U position, she was interviewing for a staff position with a local nursing home.

During Amy's interview process, she talked to some of the staff about Healing U. What she heard wasn't encouraging. Tracey, one of the nurses she would be working with, told her about the experience she had when her son broke his arm after falling off his bicycle. The emergency room was overflowing and they waited over an hour and a half to be brought into the treatment area. Not a great place to be if you're a kid already in distress. Once inside, their experience didn't improve. Tracey said that the nurses were running back and forth like chickens with their heads cut off and no one seemed to know who was assigned to her son. Could anyone give him something for pain? Was his arm broken? Who was supposed to take him to x-ray? No one seemed to have time to explain anything to her because they were too busy trying to do other things. In the end he ended up getting adequate treatment, but it was a very stressful experience on her part and especially for her son.

After our interviews that day, Amy and I debriefed on the day's events. I was intrigued by the challenge—the bigger the better for me. But I had also learned to rely on Amy's instinct, and the perspective she brings from a more nurturing point of view. I think that's what really balances us out as a couple. "Will," she said, "someone needs to turn that hospital around. I think you should do it." Her confidence and support had sealed the deal for me.

But after a month in the job, I sat there at the end of a long hard day with a sinking feeling that we may have made the wrong decision. I was very discouraged, and all the optimism with which I accepted the position currently seemed light-years away. I wondered what I had gotten myself into. I remember thinking "Do I have the ability to turn this place around? Is it even possible?" I thought about Amy and my son, Tyler. Would I be comfortable having them come to Healing U for treatment? Or would I want them to go to a competitor? I started to envision what it would be like here: waiting in the ER for hours, eventually getting upstairs to a dirty room staffed by overworked nurses. I was overwhelmed, exhausted, and feeling quite hopeless.

"Stop!" I said to myself. I can't think about it anymore. I'd had enough for one day, and headed home.

Chapter TWO

Inspiration and Hope

I entered the front door of my home, worn out and exhausted. I was greeted excitedly by our dog, Cinder. She was a little black Schipperke, all of fifteen pounds soaking wet. She jumped up and down, all the way to my knees, as she welcomed me home. Even on the worst days I could count on Cinder to be happy to see me.

Amy also greeted me, and asked me how my day went. Before I could even answer her my cell phone rang. "What now?" I wondered, thinking it was probably something at the hospital.

It was my sister, Paula. "Don't worry," she said. "Mom is OK."

"What happened?" I asked anxiously.

"Mom had a minor heart attack, but she's OK."

" When did this happen?" I asked, still reeling from the news.

"It happened this morning, about eight o'clock or so."

"And you are just now letting me know about it?" I asked incredulously.

"Check your phone," Paula said. I've been calling you all day. It immediately goes to voice mail."

"Oh," I said, realizing I had been out of my office and working in the hospital most of the day. Coverage was spotty there at best.

"Don't worry," Paula said. "She's already on the mend. And the care she received was excellent." My sister, the ever so competent ED nurse and consummate professional, observed every moment of mom's care and wanted to tell me all about it.

"Early this morning mom started experiencing chest pain and shortness of breath, and said she had a slight pain radiating up her left arm. I was worried it might be a heart attack, and called 911. They got here in just under three minutes. I told them to take her to Mercy, since they are the best hospital in town. The EMTs did a quick assessment, including a twelve-lead EKG. Fortunately, Mercy and metro EMS have worked together so that the EKG results can be forwarded to the hospital in real time; and the ER had already seen them by the time we arrived."

"Once we arrived at the ER, we were met by a professional staff nurse that gave mom immediate assistance. He began the triage process before she even entered the building. Noting the potential signs, and identifying no contradictions, he initiated an ACS (acute coronary syndrome) protocol. He introduced himself, told us that he was an RN and had been working in the ER for twelve years, and confidently assured mom that "we will take good care of you—you are in good hands."

"Paula," I interrupted, "do you have to make it so clinical? This is our mom we are talking about!"

"I'm sorry, Will, but I am an ED nurse you know. Do you want to hear about it or not?"

"Sorry. Yeah, go ahead," I said. She couldn't help herself—and with good reason. As an ED nurse she knew the exact protocols that were supposed to be followed and observed the actions the staff had taken to care for mom to ensure that they were used. I decided I needed to just be patient and let her tell me in her own words.

"The nurse was very competent. His professionalism and obvious compassion towards mom visibly lessened her anxiety, and mine. He gave mom an aspirin and a beta blocker—that's protocol you know. And as he did, he described what he was doing and why. We appreciated his warm and professional candor; and while we were still a little scared, we felt encouraged and reassured to be cared for by such a competent and caring professional.

"A technician arrived momentarily to get another EKG, which he explained would provide the doctor with additional information on how her heart was doing.

"The doc got there just moments later, as the EKG was printing out. After taking a moment to review the results, she confirmed our fears: 'I think you are having a mild heart attack.'

"But then she confidently and warmly reassured us: 'But I think you are going to be fine. Let's get you up to the heart catheterization lab where we can get in there and have a look.'"

"That must have been a relief," I said, feeling relieved myself.

"Not exactly the news we wanted to hear, but on the other hand, we were afraid it might have been much worse," my sister continued.

"Our nurse was excellent. He started an IV and gave mom a thrombolytic, which he explained would improve the circulation to her heart muscle. 'Is there anything else I can do for you right now?' he asked sincerely. There wasn't, but we were comforted by his friendliness, his warm assurance, and his confidence. Then they whisked mom off to the cath lab."

I knew enough about the protocols for AMI to know that they had done everything exactly by the book—best practice. I'm sure their quality measures were high, unlike ours.

"Before I knew it the cardiologist joined me in the waiting room. 'I've got good news,' he said. 'It is only a very minor blockage. We used a procedure called an angioplasty to eliminate it. In an angioplasty, we insert a device called a catheter into the blocked artery and using a balloon we add pressure to this area to open the blockage.' He told me they would keep mom for at least a few hours, and that if she was still doing well she could go home."

As my sister described her dialogue with the cardiologist, it struck me that he really took some time with her to explain exactly what they had done. I was fairly certain that most of our docs would not have done that.

"At that point, I got a great feeling of relief, and thanked God for hearing my prayers," continued Paula. "I walked into mom's room and asked her how she was doing. She said she was a little groggy, but wasn't feeling any pain or discomfort whatsoever. 'You should be back to your old self before you know it,' I told her."

"In the recovery area we were greeted by another nurse who introduced herself with a comforting look and the sound of reassurance in her voice. She was also very warm and professional in her approach and kept us informed of everything that she was doing. She told us that this unit specialized in care of patients after angioplasties. There was a white board on the wall, and she wrote her name on it. She assured mom that she was going to make sure she was very comfortable during her stay, and told us to let her know if there was anything at all she could do to make mom's stay more comfortable. Her sincerity convinced us that she meant every word of it. Then she fluffed mom's pillow, got her a drink of water, and asked: "What else can I do for you – I've got time" as she stood beside her near the bed.

"That afternoon Dr. Smith came by, said that everything looked great, and he was discharging mom home. Before we left, someone from Cardiac Rehab came by to make us aware of the programs they offer and gave us information on signing up based on the doctor's recommendations.

"Then mom's nurse came in and sat down with us to review her discharge instructions. Aspirin and a beta blocker were prescribed, and she also provided us with some educational material about mom's medications. Right after that, a friendly looking young man arrived with a wheel chair to take mom to the car. I brought her home, and now I am talking to you."

"Wow," I said to Paula. "Sounds like mom had a great experience! If I had to have a heart attack, that is where I would want to be treated."

"Yeah, me too." And almost as an afterthought she added "Why can't Healing U be more like Mercy?" As someone I sometimes used when I needed to vent, Paula was all too familiar with the challenges I had been facing since arriving at Healing U.

"Why indeed?" I thought. The startling news of my mom's heart attack and Paula's story about the care mom received got me thinking about Healing U a little differently. First, it became personal, in a way that it was never personal before. It was always a challenge, and always about the patients. But not personal. I began to wonder if I would feel comfortable sending my family and friends to Healing U. I thought about our ER. I thought about our heart care. Would I want mom to come here? I was sure I didn't. In fact, I realized that I wouldn't even feel comfortable having my mom come in town to visit, just in case she had another heart attack. I realized that I didn't trust Healing U well enough to take care of any of the most important people in my life.

Second, I realized that if Mercy could do it, so could we. That was my epiphany. "Wow," I thought to myself," mom had a great patient experience! That's what I want for my mom. That's what I want for all of my family and friends. That's what I want for all of our patients. And if Mercy can do it, why can't we?"

I allowed myself to imagine a vision of Perfect Care at Healing U. And having clearly envisioned it, I started to hope it was possible; and I started to believe it was possible. After all, that is why I had made health care my career. That is why I had taken this very position.

When I got off the phone with Paula, I updated Amy on my mom's situation, and the epiphany I had.

"I guess we will want to go visit your mom," Amy said. "Perhaps you could talk to the CEO while you're there and see what their secret is."

"Honey, that's a great idea," I said sincerely; again appreciating her encouragement and perspective. We complemented each other well.

Chapter THREE

It's About The People; It's About The Process

We visited mom early the next afternoon. She was recovering nicely, and would soon be back to her old self. We talked about her experience at Mercy, and like Paula, mom felt she had received excellent care. She was very comforted by the friendly and professional staff. "They sure know what they are doing there," she concluded.

At that point I was convinced of that, as well. I had done my research. Mercy was nationally renowned for heart care; a US News and World Report Top 50. They also held that distinction in neurosurgery and orthopedics. All of their core measures were at or above the 90th percentile. They never had "Never Events." They had Magnet® status for nursing and a four percent nursing turnover rate. And while I saw no data on it, I suspected their physician and patient satisfaction scores must also have been impressive, since market share had increased an average of three percent a year over the past five years. And they were making money—a solid five to six percent year in and year out. I was anxious to see what they were doing, and to see what I could learn from them. Frankly, I was a little surprised when the CEO, Paul Sage, readily agreed to meet with me.

I remember the plane ride there. I was filled with a guarded optimism, hope still tempered with doubt, but I was completely committed to turning things around at Healing U. There were so many questions. How do they do it? How do they perform so well and still make a profit? We weren't doing either very well. I wondered what kind of impressive and foreboding man Paul must have been, and the magic I would behold at their transformation.

Imagine my surprise when there was no magic! First of all, I expected a well-manicured, immaculately dressed, razzle-dazzle kind of CEO. But Paul was anything but that. He was an unassuming and soft-spoken man with a warm and friendly smile. Yet, he spoke with a quiet confidence, and the wisdom of one who has coupled his keen intellect with the knowledge of experience. His salt and pepper hair contributed to the aura of wisdom, and I discovered that Paul was well into his 60s although he could have easily passed for early 50s. As a younger CEO myself, Paul's age, experience, and track record allowed me to check my ego at the door and see what I could learn from him. Moreover, Paul seemed to have a genuine interest in Healing U and how we were doing. Only later did I understand why—health care was also a calling to him. He wanted every hospital in America to provide the same great level of care that Mercy provided.

Paul was quite the gracious host. He walked me through his hospital, and everything I observed worked like clockwork. Average length of stay (ALOS) in the ED was roughly one hour and fifteen minutes. Surgeries started on time. Their length of stay was the lowest I had seen, and most patients were discharged in the morning.

But as much as anything, I was most impressed by the interaction between the staff and their patients. There was an almost palpable healing environment created by the warmth, sincerity and caring between physicians, nurses, techs, and patients alike. You could tell the staff really wanted to be there, and they really wanted to ensure that the patients had as good care as possible. It was evident that the patients appreciated and responded in kind, just as my mother had.

By the time we got back to his office, I had lapsed from hopeful optimism to hopeless despair. There was no way Healing U was ever going to get to this level of performance, much less instill the culture they had. Paul could tell I was discouraged, and after I told him about the state of affairs at Healing U, I suspected he would want to throw in the towel as well. Instead, he began to tell me about his experience, with the same warm assurance that I saw his nurses show their patients.

"So what is your secret?" I asked. He gave a little pause, and said "It's quite simple really. It's about the people, and it's about the process. We empower our people to improve our processes."

"That's it?" I asked, neither quite believing nor understanding him at that point.

"Basically, yes," Paul said. "The most important thing that I and the other leaders do is simply maintain a focus on the effort—a constancy of purpose, if you will—and be actively engaged in finding and removing barriers to performance excellence. We have to establish the environment, ensure alignment of efforts across the system, and make sure our people have the tools to be successful. "

"Tools?" I asked. With our capital constraints, if this was about having the latest and greatest technological advancements that was not going to be a possibility.

"Sorry," said Paul. "I don't mean the latest and greatest machines and equipment. I mean the latest and greatest process improvement technologies. I'm talking about Lean. 'Tools' may not be the best word. Lean does provide a powerful set of tools to help with process improvement, for example Value Stream Mapping, Five S, Kanbans, and poka-yoke; but it is more than that. It is an approach to process improvement that focuses on improving the flow of processes by eliminating wastes in the process. We use Lean and the Lean tool kit to help us with everything from implementing our strategic plan to improving throughput in the lab."

Oh great, I think. "Yeah, I've heard about it. Lean—the latest quality improvement fad. First there was Taylor scientific management, then quality circles, then Total Quality Management, then reengineering, etc., etc.," I said; but to be honest, I really didn't know what I thought about it. I had heard both good reports and bad.

"Well," Paul said, "by whatever name, all of these are about customer focus, process improvement, leadership, and the empowerment of your people. I've given it a lot of thought, and I've come to define them this way: they are all leadership philosophies that emphasize and achieve customer satisfaction by relying on employees and statistical tools to continually improve processes. I take what tools I can from each and integrate them into my overarching constant of continual improvement."

That got my attention, so I asked him to repeat it so I could write it down:

Continual Improvement, in all its forms, is a leadership philosophy that emphasizes and achieves customer satisfaction by relying on employees and statistical tools to continually improve processes.

When he saw I was taking notes, Paul said "That is important, but it's not the most important. He repeated what was most important, so that I could write that down too:

It's about the people; it's about the process.

As I considered this, I had a bit of a nagging thought.

"But isn't it about the patient??" I asked Paul.

"Is it about the patient?" He asked rhetorically.

"It is to me," I replied.

"Me too," assured Paul. "How do we provide patient care?"

Not too well, I thought to myself, before I realized where he was going with this.

“Ah,” I said. “We provide patient care through our people and our processes!”

“Indeed we do,” concurred Paul. “And that is what we can control. As the leaders—owners, if you will—of the system, it is our responsibility to ensure that we have the best people and processes to ensure great patient care.

At that point I had had about all I could absorb for one day, and more importantly I wanted to visit mom and see how she was doing. Paul was gracious enough to let me come back for a couple hours in the morning, which worked perfectly for Amy and I to catch our early afternoon flight.

We spent a very enjoyable evening with mom and Paula. Already mom’s spirits seemed to be lifted, and she looked physically much improved. She even had a bit of dinner with us. My wife and sister, being nurses, thought mom was doing quite well, too.

I shared my day with them, including some of the highlights. Amy was encouraged and excited, and could detect the same in me.

“Will,” she said, “it sounds like you are pretty excited about what you learned. “Now you can straighten that place up,” she said, believing it. I wasn’t as confident, but another thing about Amy was that she thought more highly of me than I deserved, and her confidence motivated me to do my best not to disappoint her.

My sister wasn’t quite as optimistic. I had a history of being a bit head strong, and she knew me better than most.

“Yeah,” she said, “now if you will only take some of Paul’s advice.”

She was right. I had a lot of confidence in my own abilities and my own judgment. But I had also seen for my own eyes what Paul and Mercy had accomplished. As my dad, God rest his soul, once told me ”experience is the best teacher, but the fool will learn from no other.“ Paul had learned through experience. In spite of my strong inclination to rely on my own counsel and experience, I was going to try to check my ego at the door and learn what I could from him.

Experience is the best teacher, but the fool will learn from no other — Ben Franklin

Chapter FOUR

Experience is the Best Teacher

I returned early the next morning. If Paul wanted me to be in an optimistically but skeptically hopeful and confused state, he had me right where he wanted me. I looked forward to learning more with a mixture of respect and admiration for this thoughtful and results-oriented leader.

Thankfully, we started that morning over coffee. I was up most of the night reeling in the flurry of thoughts and images that crowded out my sleep. I wanted to know how he did it—how he transformed the organization, how he knew what to do, how he got his team on board. I had a myriad of questions. So I asked him, and Paul's answer surprised me. He said "How did I do it? I'll tell you. But before we talk about *how* to do it, it's probably more important that we talk about how *not* to do it. I'm living proof that you can set yourself up for failure just by how you choose to start. It didn't happen here, but several years ago at another hospital." Then Paul spontaneously started telling me his story.

"In my earlier days I took over leadership for a small county hospital. Total Quality Management (TQM) was in vogue at the time, and I decided I would use that to transform the organization. Suffice it to say that I made a few mistakes along the way, and that it wasn't quite the success it could have been. I resolved to learn from that effort, and have since refined an approach to continual improvement that yields a significantly higher probability of success.

"It wasn't a complete failure. We did do a few things right. Most importantly, we began to set the organizational tone for a cultural transformation. We did this by training all of our leaders in a set of materials that included process improvement and team based problem solving tools. They began to learn more about empowerment and participative leadership. This was a very significant start. Another important, and correct thing we did, was lead from the top. Our TQM efforts were initiated by our senior executives; our senior team was thoroughly trained and they, in turn, trained their direct reports.

"In retrospect, what we did was begin the cultural transformation by initiating top-down leadership development. An organization must have the support of its leadership team—from the executive suites to the front lines—to be successful. And we got that part right. Unfortunately, that was about all we did right; and it wasn't enough to overcome the myriad of challenges presented by the rest of the implementation approach. Top leadership support is a necessary, but insufficient, ingredient for organizational transformation.

That was a keeper, so I wrote it down:

Top leadership support is a necessary, but insufficient, ingredient for organizational transformation.

Paul smiled and continued. "As for what we could have done better, let's begin with how we introduced TQM to the organization. We did what a lot of organizations did, and frankly still do: we made a huge announcement to all that we were embarking on a new journey, one of empowerment and process improvement that would ensure our ongoing success. Well, you know what their reaction was: 'Oh no, here we go again.' Having survived quality circles, zero defects, scientific management, and every other so-called 'flavor of the month,' they were justifiably skeptical. We assured them that this time was different, just like we had every other time, but they remained skeptical. 'This too shall pass,' many must have thought to themselves. But we persevered, and when they saw that it was a leadership-led initiative, and that we did seem to be practicing what we were preaching, at least initially many did begin to believe, even hope, that this time things might finally be different. Unfortunately, we didn't maintain our focus. The point is that we made a grand announcement and spun-up everyone in the organization—some to a guarded optimism that we once again shattered; some to pessimism that we eventually validated; and most to a guardedly passive and unengaged attitude that did not bode well for our success. Not surprisingly, the initiative floundered and eventually failed.

What that experience taught me was this: Don't announce a grand new program to all. While a few will embrace such an announcement with hope and optimism, it can only be met with skepticism by most, and upon failing will further hinder the likelihood of the success of any future initiatives. The very act of announcing a new initiative of this magnitude may very well hasten its demise. A better approach is to start small. Provide only the necessary supportive foundation by educating the senior leadership team.

Don't announce a grand new program. Train the executive suite and then just get started.

Then select an area of your organization with a strong and committed leader, and begin there. Success here will breed success in other areas, and you will gradually roll out Lean to the rest of the organization. But instead of being "push," it will be "pull."

I hated to interrupt him, but as interesting as what he just said sounded, I didn't have a clue what he meant. "What do you mean by 'pull'?" I asked.

"Ah, sorry. It's a Lean concept that applies to process improvement, but which I've also found can be expanded to help understand organizational implementation. Just think about a rope: is it easier to "push" or "pull" it? The idea is always to "pull" things through a process, rather than push. Think about it this way: When your ED gets backed up with people waiting for beds, what is the ED or care manager doing—calling bed control or the units trying to get their patient a bed? That's a "push." What if, instead, the units were continually calling down to the ED: "Have you got a patient for us? That would be a "pull." For now, you can at least dream of that! But the point is that when implementing Lean, you want it to be held in such great esteem that it is pulled into areas by motivated leaders that see the opportunities it provides, rather than have it pushed by a leadership team to many who will resist.

Paul continued. "I had a great experience that really drove this point home. We were doing a Value Stream Analysis of our emergency department with a very committed executive and a cross-functional team from across the organization. The event radiated excitement, so much so that the Vice President of surgical services, who was not involved in the event, approached me during a break and said 'I'm so jealous!' I asked what she meant, and she said 'I want to do one of these with me and my team!' Wow! What an endorsement, and what a great lesson for me. Start in an area in which you have a great chance for success. Build some excitement, and have other leaders "pull" Lean into their areas."

> # Don't "push" Lean. Start in an area in which you have a great chance for success. Build some excitement, and have leaders "pull" Lean into their areas.

"But back to my TQM experience. Then we rolled training out to everyone—training on the philosophy, training on the tools, and training on how to work in teams. We used a train the trainer approach, cascaded from the senior executive team down. As I mentioned earlier, this did have the effect of engendering greater support, particularly of the leadership team; and it did demonstrate our commitment. But it also presented a couple of problems. The biggest problem was that we rolled out training to everyone, but everyone did not soon thereafter have an opportunity to apply what they were taught. Consequently, by the time we did ask them to engage, many had forgotten what they learned. The second problem was that when it came to training, all leaders were not equal. The cascading training approach lent itself to a huge diversity in the quality of training received."

"What I learned was this: Don't roll out training to everyone; and don't cascade training down using your leadership team. Provide training Just in Time (JIT) by qualified experts so that team members can employ what they learn immediately."

Don't roll out training to everyone at the start. Do it just in time.

"To compound the problem, once we had cascaded training down through the organization, we acted as if we had certified all the participants as master Black Belts. Without additional support or development, we told them to go out and pick a process to improve and start working on it. And some of them did. They picked a process and started working to improve it. Some were successful, but there are at least two problems with this approach. First, they may not have chosen the most important, or even a mildly important, process to improve. Second, they may have chosen a process to improve that led to system sub-optimization."

I wanted to interrupt Paul there, to ask about sub-optimization. But he went right into it, almost as if he had read my mind.

"Sub-optimization occurs when one process is improved, but its improvement does not lead to improvement of the larger containing process. In other words, part of a system is improved but the overall performance of the system does not improve. As an example, imagine that you are trying to decrease ALOS in your ED. The team, freshly trained and itching to go, decides to improve the turnaround time between the ED and the lab. They do a great job, decreasing it from 68 minutes to 42. But ALOS in the ED doesn't improve; that wasn't the bottleneck. They sub-optimized the process. They wasted their efforts improving a part of the system that did not improve the overall performance of the system."

"So my lesson learned there was this: Take a systems approach. Use a Value Stream Analysis to help identify where the leverage points of a process are. Ensure that the team works on those first. This will ensure that improvements achieved will translate to improvement of the system.

Paul was on a roll, but I had to interrupt him again: "Value Stream Analysis?"

"Sorry. I've become so used to these terms that I use them without even thinking. A Value Stream Analysis, or VSA for short, is a very intense type of process analysis, including specialized flowcharting tools, accomplished by a cross-functional team of your process workers, and facilitated by a Black Belt. A VSA and some associated tools tell you what part of the process you need to improve to get improvement in the performance of the overall process, like the ED example I just gave you. We should have made the team start with a VSA, then they would have known what part of the process to start to improve, rather than randomly selecting the interface between the ED and lab that had no impact on ALOS since it wasn't the bottleneck. In other words, we didn't assign teams strategically. We sub-optimized by letting them work on parts of the process that weren't leverage points.

Start with a Value Stream Analysis to keep from sub-optimizing. Align improvement efforts with the organization's priorities.

"Last, but not least," Paul continued, "our approach to team meetings also missed the boat. Our TQM teams typically met on a weekly basis, for one or two hours. We spent the first half of the meeting trying to remember where we left off last time. Everyone couldn't make it to every meeting. We lacked a sense of urgency and we lacked commitment. Eventually the energy and excitement would fade, commitment waned, and the team often died a slow and painful death before getting to meaningful process improvement. Those who were optimistic that things would be different this time were disappointed yet again."

"I wasn't sure how to solve that problem until I was introduced to these Lean events: VSAs and rapid improvement events, or RIEs for short. Some people call RIEs Kaizens or Kaizen Blitzes But the way they work is this: Instead of meeting for a couple hours a week ad infinitum, immerse the team in the effort at hand for three to five days, morning until the end of the day. Yes, it is very difficult to get an hour of some people's time, much less a day, much less three to five full days. But it can be done. We are doing it, and it is one of the most successful tools we have employed. My learning here was that immersing a team in the work at hand— allowing them the time to fully study, think about, develop, and implement solutions —is a far more effective improvement strategy than weekly meetings that go on until they die, often with little to show for it; more on this later. For now, be open to the idea that this is a high-yield strategy for process improvement."

Don't have improvement teams meet for just an hour or two at a time over several weeks. Use VSAs and RIEs.

Paul concluded with a summary: "The bottom line to our TQM journey was this: we never got to measurable and sustainable process and performance improvement. Our approach was not a recipe for success. It did not help us achieve what we wanted it to, what we needed it to. I resolved when I got here that we would do it differently, and we did, with much better results.

Chapter FIVE

Lean is a Cultural Transformation Tool

Paul had to step out for a moment. If it were me it would have been to put out a fire of some sort. But not for Paul. He had a much more pleasant duty: to say a few words at a celebration commemorating three of his nurses for 30 years of faithful service. Thirty years! Hmm. I'll be lucky if any of my new hires make it two years, much less thirty. Paul invited me to join him, but I was actually happy to have a few minutes to digest the important ideas he just discussed. I noticed that he introduced the lesson as what not to do; but each "don't" was accompanied by a well-learned "do."

- Don't announce a grand new program. Do train the executive suite and then just get started.
- Don't "push" Lean. Do start in an area in which you have a great chance for success. Build some excitement, and have leaders "pull" Lean into their areas.
- Don't roll out training to everyone at the start. Do it just in time.
- Don't randomly identify processes to improve. Do start with a Value Stream Analysis to keep from sub-optimizing. Align improvement efforts with the organization's priorities.
- Don't have improvement teams meet for just an hour or two at a time over several weeks. Do use VSAs and RIEs.

I thought Paul was done, but he wasn't. His most important lesson was yet to come. He rejoined me and continued:

"Now where was I? Oh yeah, the culture. We thought we had to change the culture before we could be successful with TQM and process improvement. So we did what a lot of organizations do: tell everyone we are going to change the culture."

"To help us accomplish this Herculean effort, we rolled out training to everyone as discussed above, started developing teams and team skills, and strove to develop our leaders. And all in all, we did make some slight improvements to our culture. We started to move away from command and control to a more enlightened and participative style of leadership. We began to embrace the concept of teams. (And boy did we start a lot of them. We had a team for everything: from how to manage the coffee mess to how to build a better mousetrap!)"

"That was all good. What wasn't so good, and the important lesson here, is that as part of this cultural transformation effort, we told people and teams they were empowered. We said "We are going to change the culture. We are going to empower you." We were serious and sincere. Our intentions were good. But at the same time we really didn't know what we meant by "empowerment." And some of them actually had the nerve to believe us until, of course, their team came back with suggestions that we shot out of the water. We weren't really prepared to empower people and teams to the degree we thought; and we didn't prepare them to be successful. So much for cultural transformation, and so much for our TQM process improvement efforts.

"I learned a couple things from that experience. First, the team needs to know before it begins its work what the constraints are. In other words, what it has the latitude to change and what it must accept as status quo. People and teams can accept that there are limitations. They just want and need to know them up front so that they don't waste their time and energy on ideas that will never be approved. Charters were an important part of our transformation for a number of reasons, including being a great tool for identifying, documenting, and sharing the constraints."

"Second, and even more important, you don't change the culture by saying "we are going to change the culture." You don't empower people by saying "you are empowered." And you don't change the culture before engaging in improvement efforts. You change the culture *as* you engage in improvement efforts. The act of putting people on chartered teams—and empowering them to improve their processes and performance—is how you empower people, change the culture, and achieve performance improvement. It's not 'change the culture first, and then do process improvement.' It's 'change the culture by doing process improvement.'"

"Lean is certainly about process improvement, and that is likely the reason most engage in it. But, as importantly, Lean is also a powerful cultural transformation tool! In retrospect this makes a lot of sense, since empowering people to improve their own processes certainly should improve morale, ownership, communication, and in short, improve the culture. That's why I say Lean is about the process and it is about the people. Cultural change and performance improvement go hand in hand. One feeds off the other in a self-sustaining cycle of ever increasing excellence."

"The truth of the matter is that as leaders, we change the culture by changing the way we engage, empower, trust, and listen to our employees. Lean, if implemented correctly, is an excellent vehicle for attaining a high-performance culture."

Lean is a cultural transformation tool.

To this day, that's the most I've ever heard Paul say in one sitting. It was way too much to absorb at one time, but I had a pretty good memory and paid rapt attention. Plus I took copious notes. I thanked Paul for sharing his time and lessons-learned with me. Paul wished me the best and invited me to call any time.

I stopped by mom's house to pick up Amy. Mom was doing great. Of course, with two nurses there to assist her, she should have been! I promised to call when we got home safely, and Amy and I headed for our plane.

Chapter SIX

Back to the Real World

It didn't take long for me to be drawn back into the immediate challenges facing our organization. Unfortunately, my new learnings and insights did not magically transform Healing U in my absence. I think they might have even gotten worse. When I arrived early that morning there were six surveyors in the executive conference room planning an unannounced state survey. Yes, "survey," I thought. That is just a kinder, gentler term for what it really is—an extensive audit, the success or failure of which determines our ability to treat Medicare and Medicaid patients. And at 52 percent of our patient population, without them, no hospital. "Great. This is just what I need right now," I complained to myself.

But my team was used to these events, and they were ready to go. The command post was set up, and everyone in the organization was apprised on a nearly moment to moment basis as to where the surveyors were and what they were hot on this time. This was fire fighting at its finest. If a surveyor found something in one location, we knew they would be looking for it throughout the hospital, and we made sure they didn't find more of it. Just one failure here or there was expected, but when it repeated itself throughout the organization it fell into the category of a "systemic failure" and could warrant a provisional accreditation, or worse, revocation of our accreditation altogether. We were quite experienced at ensuring that didn't happen.

Fire fighting. As I thought about it, I realized we were darn good at it. That came from doing so much of it, and that wasn't a good thing. We spent so much time doing what was important and urgent that we didn't have time for what was important, but not so urgent—like strategic planning and developing our people. Nursing staff, technicians, environmental services, and even those of us in the executive suites all pretty much went from one fire to the next. I knew that many of the fires recurred because we failed to address the underlying root cause. We treated the symptoms and not the disease. We were so busy addressing the immediate issues—finding adequate staff to replace the ones that called in, finding the right sutures for a surgery, getting a room turned over so we could get a patient moved from the ED, responding to urgent requests for meetings with physicians or, as in the current situation, dealing with unscheduled audits—that we never had time to resolve the underlying cause. It was quite overwhelming. Another vicious cycle.

The surveyors were waiting for me in the conference room. I greeted them, thanked them for being here, and told them I looked forward to their objective evaluation. I assured them that we were always trying to improve, and that their feedback would provide valuable information about where the opportunities were. That's what I said, and I really meant it—sort of. They were very knowledgeable people, and coming from outside our system they could provide objective and meaningful feedback. But in my stressed and overwhelmed state I was also thinking about how glad I would be when it was over and they were out of there. I left them to their work and went to see why we were already backed up in the imaging department again that morning.

Why were we backed up? We had just put in place a new policy to try to alleviate some of the issues there. I went down and to my amazement saw that although we were backed up, one of our CT scanners was idle, and with a full staff standing by to boot! I asked them why it wasn't being used.

"In their infinite wisdom scheduling decided we needed to leave some slots open for add-ons," the tech told me.

I called the scheduling manager to see what was going on. "Well, Will, we had a big problem in scheduling. About 23 percent of our cases are physicians' offices calling in wanting a stat CT. Before, the only thing we could do was squeeze them in or tell them we couldn't accommodate them. And since we are really trying to drive up our volume we didn't want to turn them away. So we decided to have some slots earmarked especially for stats. Our scheduling process has been so much easier that way. When a doc's office calls and needs a stat, we put them in the slot we have reserved."

I about went ballistic. "So let me see if I understand this," I said. "We are trying to increase our patient volume. So to make sure we can add a patient to the schedule in case of a stat, we don't schedule a patient to that slot in advance." I was incredulous, and he didn't get it. Of course, from his perspective, he had solved a problem. What he didn't see was the problem caused elsewhere, and the impact on the overall system. That is exactly what Paul was talking about when he was telling me about sub-optimization. We had fixed one part of the process only to have a negative impact on the overall process. I took note of yet another opportunity for improvement.

The out-brief for the survey late that afternoon wasn't pretty. There were some supplies in the OR supply room that had expired, so now everywhere they went they were looking at expiration dates. They didn't like the clutter in one of the labs. They found dust on CT2. The truth was, they were going to find something, and these weren't show-stoppers. The problems they found with our Policies and Procedures were much more serious, however. They initially wanted to see our policy for abuse reporting, and asked the nurse manager in several different areas for a copy. Most at least had a copy, but the problem was they weren't all the same revision. One version was over six years old and was about four revisions behind the current one.

This put them on a high alert for other policy and procedure violations. Unfortunately, they found plenty of them. As with the abuse reporting procedure, they found occurrences of other policies and procedures either missing or with multiple versions floating around. These included our policies on infection control, patient falls, life safety violation reporting, and patient complaint escalation procedures. Even more disconcerting, our practices were not consistent. Not only did we not follow the same procedures on main campus as we did at our ambulatory sites, but the second shift didn't even do things the same way the first shift did. Suffice it to say, by the time they had completed their report it was clear that this was a systemic issue. And this was just day one of what would likely be a five-day survey.

As I walked back to my office, my initial response was to be defensive. "They've got to find something, that's their job," I thought to myself. But I couldn't stop the nagging feeling that their findings were valid, and truth be told, just the tip of the iceberg. Truth was, we had some problems. Patient charts, or at least parts of them, went missing. We measured, in inches, the number of loose pages that we couldn't match with a patient. We either didn't get or lost physician orders, which meant we had to either go through a heck of a lot of rework to get them, or we didn't get paid. Nursing units often got the wrong supplies due to bad ordering templates. We didn't seem to rotate our stock very well, and consequently had expired inventory. Plus, our supply system was so unreliable that nurses kept a whole warehouse full of supplies tucked away in their drawers and cabinets so they didn't run out. I didn't blame them— they wanted to make sure they had what they needed for their patients' care—but it was costing us a fortune in supply costs.

These were all symptoms of the underlying problem: we didn't have standardized policies and procedures; and when we did, we didn't follow them consistently. This created an enormous amount of waste and rework, and unsatisfactory patient care provided at a higher cost. "Higher cost, lower quality," I thought to myself, sarcastically. I don't think that's the way it is supposed to work.

Higher Cost, Lower Quality???

Late Friday afternoon we had the final out-brief for the survey. My team and I were a bit more worried than usual, and waited expectantly for the bottom line. Was our accreditation to be renewed or not? We had to wait for them to go through each finding, one at a time. At the end of the day, there were seventeen areas of incomplete compliance with standards, eight of which were deemed "direct impact" and the balance "indirect impact." I understood it a lot better when they just said "majors" and "minors," but as it turned out, we provisionally maintained our accreditation and our licensure was not in jeopardy. We had sixty days to submit "evidence of standards compliance," and no requirement for a resurvey. We were greatly relieved.

Relieved, but not nearly satisfied. In my short tenure as CEO I had already seen way too many opportunities for improvement: fire fighting, stovepipes, workarounds, inadequate policies and procedures, and inconsistent adherence to them. All things considered—what I had witnessed myself, what our physicians and patients were telling us, and the results of the survey—we were broken, and it was going to take a lot of work to make us whole. Fighting the urge to despair, I recalled the experience mom had at Mercy and my visit with Paul. Based on our short time together I had some ideas on how to begin, and I resolved to bounce them off of him first thing in the morning.

I called it a day and headed home. I pulled into the driveway, relieved that my workday was over, and hopeful that I might recharge my batteries before fighting the fires of tomorrow. My next door neighbor Martha was getting out of her car. Martha and her husband Gary had gotten to be pretty good neighbors in the short time Amy and I had lived here, and I greeted her with a warm hello.

"Hey Will," she said, seeming a bit frazzled.

"Everything OK," I asked?

"Well, hopefully it will be. I just left Gary to spend the night in your hospital.

"What happened?" I asked, concerned.

"Gary had to have his appendix removed. The docs say he will be fine."

I was relieved that Gary didn't have anything too serious, and that he was going to be OK. "How did we do," I asked with trepidation.

"Will," she said bluntly "to be honest, it was a horrible experience. I took him in late last night. First off, they were so backed up that it took forever to get him in to be looked at. Once they finally did, the doctor was really rude to him and no one seemed to want to do anything for the pain. There was plenty of staff milling about, but it seemed like no one paid him much attention. Once we got inside we sat in a room for five hours waiting for docs, tests, and test results. They finally decided it was his appendix, but couldn't get to the surgery until today!"

This seemed like deja vu all over again. It was a lot like the story my wife heard from her friend Tracey when her son came here with a broken arm. I definitely wouldn't want anyone I knew to come to Healing U in case of an emergency, and this was just another confirmation of that sad fact. I apologized to Martha, and although I knew it was too little too late, acknowledged our challenges in the ER and told her it was a priority for me.

Chapter SEVEN

The Healing Way

Paul was his usual cheery self when I called. He was just returning from a press conference to announce that their Magnet® status had just been reaffirmed. "Rub it in," I thought to myself. We can barely pass a survey to maintain our accreditation; much less qualify for Magnet®.

"So what's going on?" Paul asked.

I didn't wait for him to ask twice, and launched right in. I told him about our survey, the fire fighting, the stove piping, the OR being backed up, all of our work-a-rounds, and the confounding issue of keeping the schedule open now so we could fill it later. I told him about my neighbor Gary and his experience in our ER.

Paul listened patiently and must have detected my frustration, perhaps bordering on hopelessness. When I was done he empathized with me, and said he knew exactly how I felt.

"Sounds like you are about where I was when I took the helm," said Paul.

I was encouraged as he reminded me that he too had faced a similar situation, and had emerged victoriously from it.

Then, recognizing the fruitlessness of dwelling on the imperfect present, he asked what I knew was a leading question. (Paul was well versed in employing the Socratic method.) He asked me whether I thought these were an independent set of problems, or whether they might all be symptoms of an underlying cause.

That was the exact question I had been struggling with, especially after hearing the results of our survey. I had come to the conclusion that in fact these were all symptoms of an underlying set of systemic issues. I laid it out for Paul as I saw it:

- Healing U has not fully developed, integrated, and implemented standard policies, procedures and processes across the system; much less best practices.

- Where policies and procedures do exist, there is inconsistent adherence to them.
- This results in patient safety and liability issues, challenges to accreditation status, stove-piped and sub-optimized processes, and systemic inefficiencies leading to poor financial performance.

"Well said, grasshopper," Paul observed with what I sensed was a smile in his voice. "I would add one more point to your list:

- A lack of standardized processes makes it difficult for an organization to hard-wire process improvements

"Interesting," I said. "Tell me more."

Paul told me to hold on a second, sent me an email, and once I had received it started to explain. "I know you are familiar with the PDCA cycle: Plan, Do, Check, Act. Without considering the details of the cycle for now, just think of it as a model for a continual improvement process. Continual turns of the PDCA wheel roll it up a ramp towards ever improving patient care and financial performance. The more continual improvement work you do— i.e., the more turns of the wheel, the better your performance."

He continued. "Standard policies and procedures, and the standardized processes they foster, are the chock block that help you hold your gains and keep you from rolling backwards. Without the organizational discipline of such standardized processes, you will not be able to hold the gains and the PDCA wheel will slip backwards down the ramp.

Standard Policies and Procedures

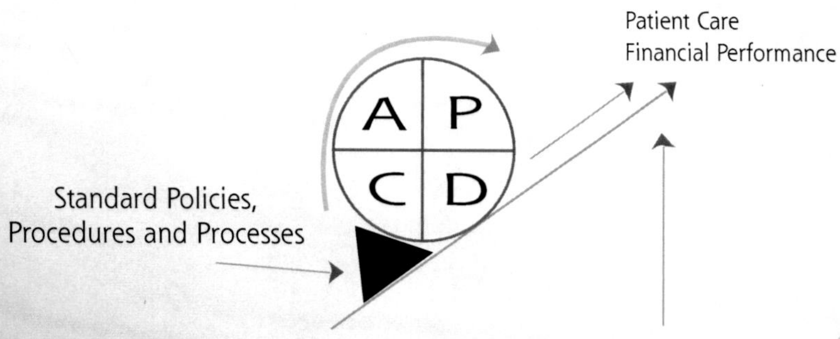

"That's very interesting," I thought out loud. "Can you tell me more about that?"

"Sure. Remember me telling you about my experience with total quality management? W. Edwards Deming was the guy that started that for the most part, and is also the one who popularized the PDCA cycle. He said that before you try to improve your system, it needs to be stable. He said that trying to improve an unstable system is just 'meddling.'"

Trying to improve an unstable system is just meddling
— Paraphrase of W. Edwards Deming

"I have given that a lot of thought over the years," Paul continued, "and here is how I have come to think about it: Trying to improve an unstable system is like building on sand. We need to treat our hospital system like we do our critical patients. We try to stabilize them first. Then we look at improving their health."

"Think about it like this. Let's say your nurses on second shift in the ED don't do things exactly like the nurses on first shift. Even worse, let's say there is variation from nurse to nurse on a given shift. As an example, imagine that whenever one of them needs to draw blood they draw several tubes worth, just in case; and another only draws what is needed. They do things differently. First of all, that means that they are not all using best practice. Second, if you don't have the organizational discipline to do basic processes, like drawing blood the same way—in other words, if behavior changes from individual to individual—what are the chances of redesigning a process and getting everyone to follow the new procedure? Not high."

"So there are really two separate but interdependent concepts. You identified the first in your list of items: standard policies and procedures, and consistent adherence to them. I call that the quality management system. It is the stable system provided by documented policies and procedures that yield consistent and standardized processes. The second is continual improvement. We are applying Lean as our continual improvement approach. So if you look at my drawing again, you could think about it like this:

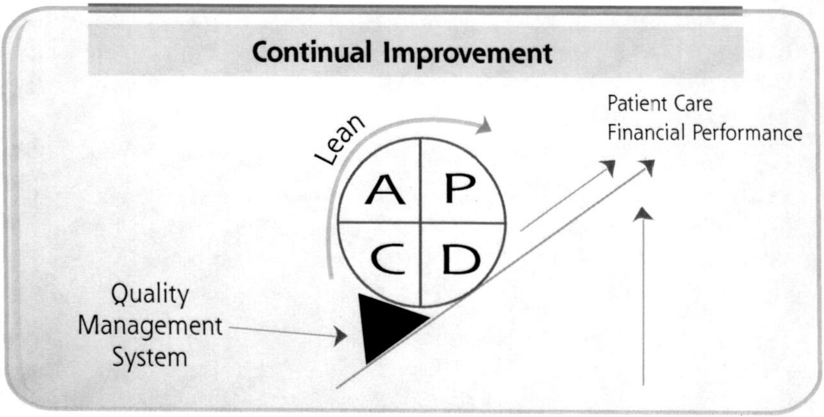

It took me a few minutes to digest what Paul was saying, and when I thought I had it I repeated it back to him. "So, we achieve a stable system by implementing a quality management system as the foundation. Then we improve this stable system by applying Lean to continually improve patient care and financial performance?"

"Exactly," Paul agreed.

This conversation with Paul started to help me crystallize the two separate but interdependent pieces of the performance improvement puzzle. You've got to have standardized, repeatable, reliable processes as the foundation. Then you apply Lean tools to improve those processes. Simple enough.

As I thought about it, it began to make a whole lot of sense. The basic Quality Management System is what provides the stable foundation. Its basic requirement is to "Say what you do and do what you say." That was a very simple and succinct statement, and yet so full of meaning and challenge. Whatever it is you are supposed to do, you need to document it, teach it, and ensure that it continues to be done that way.

Even in the absence of continual improvement, a stable system alone would ensure safe and reliable delivery of health care to our patients. After all, what is it that causes sentinel events—that is, serious events that result in death or serious injury to our patients, not related to the natural course of the patient's illness? Nine times out of ten it is lack of adherence to a documented process, for whatever reason. Sometimes the process is not documented; sometimes there is human error; sometimes there is simply neglect to follow the documented process.

I had recently read an article about the reliability of commercial air travel and naval aviation. It is amazing how safe air travel is. In contrast, I recalled the alarming statistic we learned from *To Err is Human*, from the Institute of Medicine: there are as many as 100,000 deaths per year due to medical errors. I wondered how many airplane crashes that would be. Let's say there are about 300 people on an average wide body flight. That's the equivalent of 333 jumbo jets crashing per year, killing all the passengers on board! As a country, as a culture, we certainly would not tolerate that. And yet we allow up to 100,000 accidental deaths per year in those institutions entrusted with healing!

Returning from my flight of fancy, I re-engaged in my conversation with Paul, and asked for his thoughts around the parallels between safety in aviation and healthcare. Paul really honed in on the use of standard procedures and checklists.

"We are all familiar with the stereotype of pilots before takeoff going through their checklists: 'Flaps down? Check. Pressure gauges? Check. Engines? Check. Cockpit? Check. Cabin? Check....' It is part of their training and their culture. And it has gotten results. Air travel is orders of magnitude safer than a visit to one of our hospitals. It is due to their training and disciplined adherence to procedures and checklists."

"And it has been shown to work in healthcare," Paul continued, "I recently came across a New England Journal of Medicine Article about that. The use of a 19-item surgical safety checklist resulted in significant improvements in rates of death and inpatient complications. Tracking nearly 4000 surgical patients, rate of death decreased 47 percent over baseline; and inpatient complications decreased 36 percent. Many hospitals have begun to deploy checklists with this same level of success."

"OK – I think I've got it," I said to Paul. "First we need to ensure that we have documented procedures. Then we have to make sure team members are rigorously trained, both as individuals and as teams, and that they are competent and confident in their ability to masterfully perform their responsibilities. We need to incorporate checklists and a culture of relying on them in patient safety related areas. That will provide us with a stable system, upon which we can start to drive continual performance improvement."

"You've got it," said Paul. "And of course, it's not only patient safety that will improve. By really focusing on developing your people, documenting procedures, ensuring they are fully deployed through training and ongoing assessment, and ensuring the disciplined use of checklists and standardized protocols, your process variation will decrease. This will yield improvements in throughput and financial performance as well as patient care."

Decreased variation. Yes, that would be important. I encouraged Paul to continue.

"OK," he said. "Just one more illustration to complete the picture."

He shot me another email, with three figures in it, depicting: a system out of control, a system in control, and an improved system in control.

"Let's take another example. Let's pretend you collected some data on turnover time after the first case of the day for each of seventeen days. We'll plot them on a control chart. There is an upper control limit, or UCL, and a lower control limit, or LCL. These are calculated based on the performance of the system, and the point is that when there are data points that fall above or below the control limits, the system is out of control."

"Look at the 'system out of control chart.' Each dot represents the turnover time after the first case for a given day. The average for those seventeen days is 93 minutes, but there is significant variation from day to day: some much longer than 93 minutes and some less. And a number of points are outside the control limits. This system is out of control, most likely due to a lack of standardized processes that are consistently followed."

"So whether an average of 93 minutes is good or not, this inconsistent system will still cause you a lot of trouble. For example, how do you know when to schedule your second case of the day? One day the room is ready in 80 minutes, but on another it may take over two hours. If you said, well on average it takes 93 minutes, so we'll allow for that much time in the schedule, then on some days you have the staff waiting with nothing to do; and on other days you could be backed up for the rest of the day."

I didn't quite understand the chart yet, but I knew all too well what Paul was talking about. Our OR turnover time was not at all consistent. Add that to the fact that most days our first case didn't start on time either, and what we usually had was a backlog all day long. Surgeries were late, patients were dissatisfied, and so were physicians who couldn't afford to stand around waiting for us to get their patients' ready for surgery. This led to a vicious cycle in which we were usually late getting the patient ready, so the surgeons figured there was no need to get there on time, and so even when we were ready in all likelihood the physician wasn't. So in addition to poor patient and surgeon satisfaction, our surgical teams chronically worked overtime as the delays caused cases to continue late into the day. This was a patient and team member dissatisfier in addition to being quite costly.

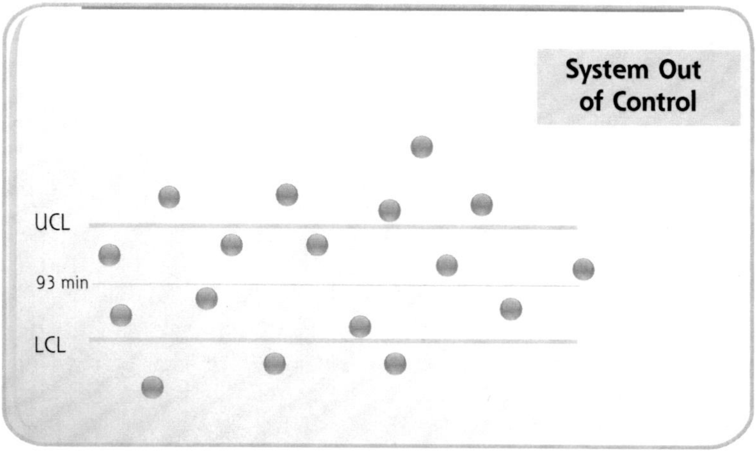

"I'm with you Paul," I said. "That is a huge problem."

"It was for us," continued Paul. "And not just in the surgical area. All throughout the hospital system, inconsistent adherence to policies and procedures creates process variation that reverberates through the system, creating delays, dissatisfaction and inefficiency. So the first thing you have to do is establish a stable system. You need to document your expected practices, then ensure consistent adherence by everyone to that process. When you do that you will get a control chart that looks something like this:

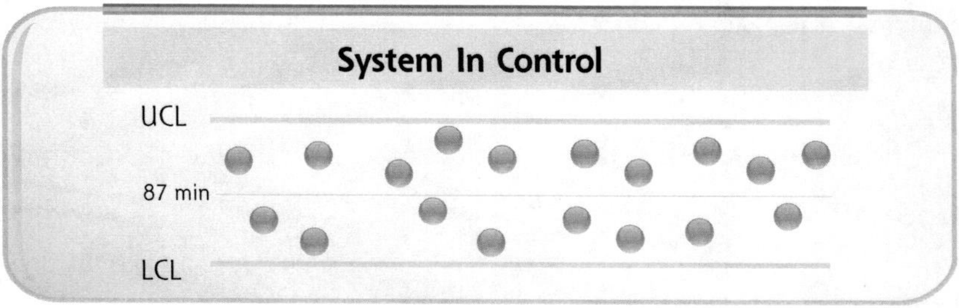

"Note that now there are no times outside the control limits. This means that your process is now more predictable—and that's the most important point. Standardizing processes is how you achieve a stable system. But you also get a little bonus for your efforts. Notice that the average turnover time has also decreased somewhat, to 87 minutes. Stabilizing a system usually results in some degree of improvement, even in the absence of intentional improvement efforts.

As soon as he said it, I got exactly what Paul was talking about. It just made sense. Going back to his surgical scheduling example, with the system in control we would have some confidence that our next case start time would be a lot closer to the average of 87 minutes. We would have less waste, less delay, less dissatisfaction, and less cost.

"Once you have achieved a stable process, you can start to apply the Lean toolkit to drive process improvement. Your aim is to achieve best practice consistently and predictably. Then your control chart will look something like this:

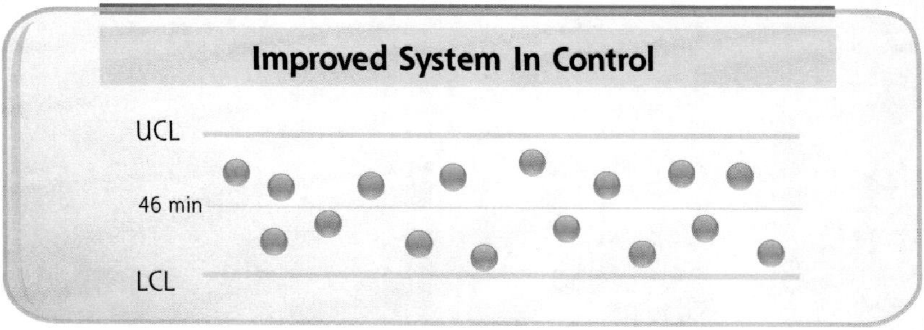

"There are two things to notice about this one. First, the average has been significantly decreased. Second, the control limits are much narrower than they were before. Your process is both improved and more predictable. If you can do that to processes across your organization, you've found the way to success."

"The Way," I thought to myself in a keen flash of insight. I said to Paul with more than a modicum of excitement: "I get it. We have to define the way we are going to do things, and ensure consistent adherence across the system. Once we have done that, we'll apply Lean to continually improve our processes. That is the way we are going to reinvent Healing U. I'm going to call it "The Healing Way."

"I like it," Paul said with a smile, and I knew he got the double entendre.

Then I wrote down the following thoughts to remind me along the way—the Healing Way!

- We need a stable system
- Say what you do and do what you say
- Standard Policies & Procedures
- Education & Training
- Checklists
- Culture of Compliance

Chapter EIGHT

Selecting our First Lean Transformation Project

I was pumped up and ready to go. Paul had said a Value Stream Analysis was the starting point, but I still didn't really know what that meant. I knew we were going to have to do some training. I knew we were going to have to identify and document our processes to achieve a stable system. And I knew we were then going to apply Lean to help us identify and achieve opportunities for improvement. How to start was the big question in my mind.

I recalled what Paul said his most important lesson was: it's about the people; it's about the process. If I was going to stabilize the system and improve processes across the organization, I was going to have to engage our people. At that point, I was tempted to go hire a consulting firm to help us roll it out, but I needed to talk it through with Paul first.

"Good Morning," I said.

"Good morning to you too!" Paul said cheerfully. He was his usual self that morning: unassuming and humble, yet with a quiet assurance that gave you the impression he knew what he was talking about. And as always, he was willing to share the hard-won fruits of his experience, and I appreciated that. It was always encouraging and motivating for me to talk with him, not to mention the clarity I achieved through our conversations.

"I think I'm ready to get started," I said.

Paul could tell I was excited, and asked me how I planned to proceed.

"Well," I replied, "based on what we've discussed before, I need to get senior leadership commitment, engage my people, do some just in time training, and just get started. But I have a couple questions about that. Early on you said "don't announce a grand new program, and don't roll out training to everyone." Are you also implying that we get started with a pilot, rather than roll out Lean across our organization all at once? I'm not sure I have the patience for that. I know I want to do this. I want us to fully engage in this process because I see it as the way—the Healing Way—to transform Healing U. But based on what you've said before, I'm guessing you would advise a more moderate start.

"Ah, such exuberance," said Paul. "Yes, I would recommend you start with a pilot first. For a number of reasons. The first is that you want to be strategic about how you roll it out across the organization. That requires some additional development and planning with your senior team, which will take some time. If you start with a pilot, so long as you choose wisely, you can literally get started within a couple weeks."

That's a good point, I thought to myself. I could get started almost immediately using Paul's approach.

"Another very important reason is that you want others in the organization to 'pull' Lean into their areas. Remember the discussion we had about that? You don't want this to be perceived as just another 'flavor of the month.' If your team hits a home run with their first project, other leaders in the organization will want to apply Lean in their areas as well. So rather than you 'pushing' it on them, they will be asking for it. That's what you want."

"Lastly, both you and Healing U will learn a lot by doing a pilot. You will make mistakes, have some missteps. And you will be able to incorporate lessons-learned from the pilot should you choose to move forward. For all these reasons, in my opinion, it is better to do a pilot. As I learned from an old mentor of mine: Do a little; learn a lot."

As usual, Paul made a compelling argument. In addition, I recalled my commitment to try to learn from his experience rather than be my normal bull in a china shop. Paul had "been there, done that," and I had no rational reason not to follow his advice. So in spite of my strong commitment to transform the organization in one fell swoop, Paul convinced me to start with a pilot. I scribbled in my notepad:

\# Do a little, learn a lot.

"OK," I said. "I'll start with a pilot. How about the ED? I've seen first-hand our problems there, including my neighbor's bad experience. The ED's our front door, and we're always on diversion, we can't get patients into beds, morale is horrible, turnover is—well, it's just a mess. If we could fix that it would be a great success story.

"Perhaps," Paul said hesitantly. "But before we get into selecting your first project, can we shift gears a bit and talk a little about your senior leadership team?"

"Uh, OK," I said hesitantly, not exactly sure where Paul was going with this.

"In my view," began Paul, "leadership is the single most important key to success. You won't be able to do this alone. You will need your senior execs to be actively engaged. Think about some of our discussions: it's about the people; it's about the process. These are your people, the people you lead. They in turn will help lead the transformation."

I hadn't really thought about it that way before. Whenever Paul said "it's about the people, it's about the process," I was always thinking about the nurses, techs, docs and everyone else in the organization. But I wasn't really thinking about me or my own team.

"That interesting," I said pensively.

"It is," said Paul. "Your role is to lead through your leaders. Just as you want them to lead and develop the people and organizations under them, so you must do with them."

"I see your point," I said, and I did. It made perfect sense. I had to lead through my leadership team. And I would want one of them to lead the first project – the one that would be most engaged and help ensure an initial success.

I inherited all of my direct reports. After just a few short months in the job I was still assessing them as individuals and as a team. I had drawn some tentative conclusions about them, but for the most part, I was still focusing primarily on the positives. I'm a strong believer in the power of expectations and the environment to influence behavior, so at that time I was expecting only the best.

Don Baird was the Chief Nursing Officer. He had been with Healing U for a little over five years. Before that he worked for both non-profits and for-profits, in a variety of different roles. Baird made a great first impression on me. He was brilliant in some ways. He had a great memory, knew every physician in town, and had a great knowledge of the industry. He seemed to be the creative, "out-of-the-box" thinker that we needed. He spoke ardently of open communication and teamwork, and was a strong vocal supporter of process improvement activities. He might also be a good candidate for our first project, and as luck would have it, he had the ED under him.

Tim Wessel was our Chief Operating Officer. He had been with the system for over five years, and before that had worked his way up the ladder, with assignments on both the operations and finance sides of the business. He knew the business well. Tim was hard working, intelligent, and steady. Highly ethical and guided by a strong moral compass, he saw his career as a calling. He was well-respected by staff and physicians for his unwavering commitment to patients and improving their care. In meetings, he did a lot of listening. He didn't speak often, but when he did, people listened. His thoughtful and well-considered comments often got right to the heart of the matter, and suggested a way forward that was often embraced by the team. Yes, Tim was solid. Part of that came by sticking with what he knew, and what worked for him in the past. I wasn't sure he was the right leader for the first project, although I knew he would get on board if we could demonstrate Lean's value.

Lana Davis was the CFO. She had been with Healing U for about a year. Before that she was CFO of a community hospital in Edgewater. Lana seemed to be very competent in all aspects of her job. She knew the numbers side, got along well with board members, and was a strong leader that did not shy away from making difficult decisions, including getting the right people on and off her team. Like Tim, Lana was also very ethical and guided by a strong moral compass. I could count on Lana to get the job done, and done well. In her previous position at Edgewater she had actually been involved with some Lean improvement projects, one in the revenue cycle area, and was a strong believer in its benefits. Lana would likely embrace our Lean efforts, and might be a good candidate for the first project.

Dr. Maggie Salmon was the Chief Medical Officer. Until recently she was a practicing neurologist—and a good one at that. As a physician, Healing University was her preferred hospital and she had been practicing here for over fifteen years. Recently she felt a calling to move into a leadership role, with a passion for improving patient care. She was dedicated and hardworking, often starting her day at 0700 with physician meetings and working late into the evening. She was also a feisty competitor, and wasn't afraid to mix it up with the docs, particularly on matters of patient care. She would be a valuable asset as we tried to improve our clinical quality, but that probably wasn't where we would start.

Denise Mariner was our Chief Administrative Officer. She had been with Healing U for over thirty years, working her way up the ladder from a front line nurse by progressively taking on additional challenges and responsibilities. Denise was also hard-working, respectful of authority, and strictly chain-of-command. She had responsibility for IT, Supply Chain, HR, and Engineering. If I needed something done, she was currently my go-to. I knew if I asked her to lead the Lean project she would salute with a "Yes, sir," and do her best to make it happen. But what I really wanted for the first project was a leader with some passion about the work. So she probably wasn't the one to start with either.

After reviewing my team with Paul, I resumed right where I left off. "So, I'm still thinking the ED. I think Baird is the kind of leader we need for our first project. That could really be a home run."

"Yes it could," agreed Paul. "I've seen organizations start with the ED for that very reason. Unfortunately, most fail. In my opinion that would be a very challenging process to start with, regardless of the executive in charge."

I didn't like where this was going, and offered a feeble protest: "But it's a pretty straight forward process."

But Paul had been there. "If it is such a straight forward process, why haven't you fixed it already?" he asked rhetorically. "At first glance it may appear to be a fairly straightforward process—registration, triage, nurse assessment, physician evaluation, treatment—but as you have seen with your own eyes, it can be quite complex. When you consider that the ED interfaces with the lab, radiology, transportation, and the inpatient units, making improvements there is actually quite complicated. Improving patient flow within an ED is actually a complex improvement process requiring a cross-functional team and the commitment of the entire organization. I understand why you want to start there, but I would certainly recommend against it."

I was disappointed, but was again swayed by Paul's wisdom and his experience. Then he asked me another question that sealed the deal.

"And by the way," he said, "let me ask you a question—what's your biggest problem in the ED?"

The answer was that the ED was often backed up and on diversion because we couldn't get the patients that needed to stay with us into beds. Patients sometimes waited ten to twelve hours or more to get to their rooms once we had made the determination to admit them.

"So your biggest problem in the ED is not really in the ED?" asked Paul.

"I guess not," I said, seeing his point. "So you're saying I should start with the nursing units and getting patients to the floors faster?"

"That would be better than starting in the ED, but that is also quite a complex process. I would recommend you not start with a patient care process. There's too much potential for adverse impact. Start on something a little more benign."

"Benign," I repeated. "Well, I don't know about benign, but our revenue cycle sure needs some help. Physicians complain they can't get patient's scheduled in a timely manner, and they say we lose orders. Our A/R days are in the sixty-five range; and cash is under a hundred days. Lana is focused on improving that, and she has had some prior experience with Lean. Maybe we could start there."

"Probably still a little too ambitious," Paul replied, "particularly without active and perseverant leadership. But it really depends on the priority that you and the leader of that area give it. You sound pretty positive on Lana. If she would be a proactive participant, that could be a crucial success factor. But here is the single most important success factor, especially for this first project—you have to stay personally involved, help maintain focus, eliminate barriers, and encourage Lana and the team. If you do that, you can make it a success. And at least any bumps you experience along the way won't directly impact patient care."

Excellent, I thought to myself with more than a modicum of building excitement. We've got a project and a leader that I think would embrace the opportunity – the Revenue Cycle. Now we can get started. "I guess I need to brief my senior team first?" I asked Paul.

"Certainly," he replied. "I think you need to let them know what you are up to, including a high level overview of Lean, Value Stream Analysis, and why you want to do it. I don't think you need to spend more than an hour or two. You really just want them to have a high level understanding of the process, and get their agreement and commitment to the pilot project. You'll want them to observe—with some curiosity—the process and outcome of this first project, so periodic updates would be useful as well. Remember, you want them to 'pull' improvement projects into their areas based on the success of this pilot."

He's beating that like a drum, I thought. That idea of leaders pulling Lean into their areas rather than having it pushed upon them. But since I couldn't argue with his results, I wasn't going to argue with his logic.

"OK," I said, "I get it. So now am I ready to do a value stream analysis?"

"Yes, I think you are," said Paul, and again I could hear the smile in his voice.

I can do that, I thought to myself unconvincingly. "OK Paul, how am I going to do that?"

"It's probably time for you to bring in some outside help," he replied. "Given that you are just now learning this yourself, you should learn the process from a wise and experienced teacher. In this business they call them Senseis or Master Black Belts. I don't get too caught up in titles, so I just call them Black Belts. I think it would be wise for you to get one to help you with this first project. After that you can decide whether you want to build your own internal team or continue to use people from the outside."

"Thanks Paul," I said. "I'll let you know how it goes."

"Any time," Paul said in his usual, sincere and friendly tone. "Have fun with it!"

Chapter NINE

Transformation 101: My Initial Lean Learnings

I was willing to learn "on the fly," but I still wanted some idea of where we were going. I knew I would have a better learning experience if I at least had a model in my mind, on which I could integrate learning. So before we did our first VSA, I asked our Black Belt consultants to give me a brief overview. I was going to call Paul, but I decided that at some point I needed to start learning for myself. I took a lot of notes at that first meeting.

Process – a set of steps that transform one or more inputs into one or more outputs. One simple example of a process is that of a nurse drawing blood from a patient. An example of a more complex process is the treatment of a patient in the ED.

Value Stream – a composite set of one or more processes that result in the delivery of a product or service. Value Streams are typically high level, or macro processes. For example, an emergency department from the point at which a patient enters until discharged is a value stream. Value streams are typically composed of multiple processes.

Value Stream Analysis (VSA) – The process of analyzing a value stream. Value Stream Analysis is a powerful tool for analyzing clinical and business processes within a healthcare system, and identifying opportunities for improvement. The analysis typically occurs during a 2-3 day event which is referred to as a VSA Event, or simply a VSA. It is a structured and facilitated event during which a cross-functional team progresses through an orderly set of steps, beginning with the current state, and ultimately yielding a plan for achieving a desired future state.

There are five fundamental components to any Value Stream Analysis.

- Set it up
- Understand the Current State
- Envision an Aspirational Ideal State
- Design an Achievable Future State
- Develop and Execute a Rapid Improvement Plan to achieve the Future State

Rapid Improvement Plan – a plan for transforming the current state of a value stream or process to the desired future state. A rapid improvement plan will typically identify multiple "Just Do Its," "Rapid Improvement Events," and "Projects," as depicted in the figure below. It will also identify who is responsible for leading each effort, and a date by when it will be completed.

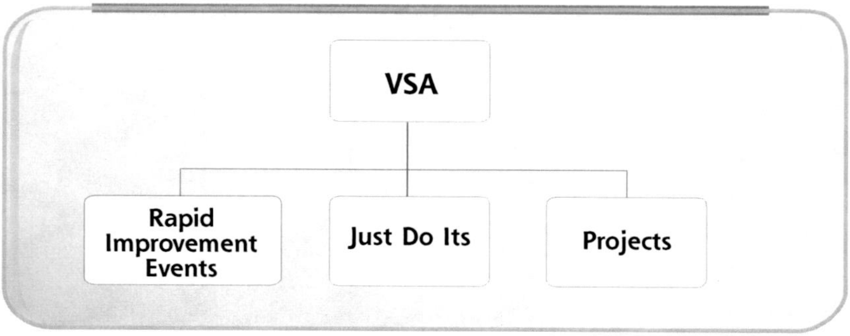

Rapid Improvement Event (RIE) – Sometimes referred to as a Kaizen. A rapid improvement event is typically a 3-5 day, facilitated event, aimed at further refining and actually implementing improvements to portions of a value stream.

Just-Do-It (JDI) – A Just-Do-It is an action for which no additional study or decision making is necessary. The team has decided it should be done, and all that is left is for someone to make it happen.

Project – an improvement effort which typically involves data analysis, and is often conducted by an engineer or small team to determine the best approach for achieving a desired outcome. Projects include Six Sigma Projects, Visual Management, Mistake Proofing, Kanban Systems, and Set Up Reduction.

Value Added Activity – Activities performed during the production or delivery of a product or service that increase its value to the customer.

Non Value Added Activity – Activities performed during the production or delivery of a product or service that utilize time or resources, but do not increase its value to the customer. There are two types of Non Value Added Activities. The first type are those activities that are "non-value added but required," due to regulatory, legal, or other requirements. The second type are those activities that are "non-value added" and not required. This second type is also called "Waste."

Waste – Activities performed during the production or delivery of a product or service that utilize time or resources, but do not increase value to the customer, and that are not required for legal, regulatory, or other reasons. There are eight types of Waste, the first letter of each forming the mnemonic "DOWNTIME":

Defects	Work that contains errors, rework, mistakes or lacks something necessary
Overproduction	Producing more than the customer needs right now
Waiting	Idle time created when material, information, people, or equipment is not ready
Not Utilizing People's Abilities	Not using people's mental, creative and physical abilities
Transportation	Movement of product that does not add value
Inventory	More materials, parts, or products on hand than the customer needs right now
Motion	Movement of people or machines that does not add value
Excess Processing	Effort that adds no value from the customer's viewpoint

Examples of the Eight Wastes in HealthCare

- **Defects** – Medication error. Wrong patient. Wrong procedure. Missing information. Redraws. Poor clinical outcomes.
- **Overproduction** – Drawing too many samples. Extra tests.
- **Waiting** – Waiting to see a doc. Waiting for a procedure. Waiting for a bed. Waiting for testing. Waiting for test results. Waiting for lab results. Waiting for discharge.
- **Not Utilizing People's Abilities** – No empowerment. "Check your brains at the door" mentality. Old school thinking, politics or the culture. Poor hiring practices. Low or no investment in training. High turn-over.
- **Transportation** – Moving samples. Moving specimens. Moving patients for testing. Moving patients for treatment. Moving equipment.
- **Inventory** – Pharmacy stock. Lab supplies. Samples. Specimens waiting analysis. Paperwork in process.
- **Motion** – Searching for patients. Searching for meds. Searching for charts. Gathering tools. Gathering supplies. Handling paperwork.
- **Excess Processing** – Multiple bed moves. Multiple testing. Excessive paperwork. Unnecessary procedures.

5S – A 5S (Sort, Set in Order, Shine, Standardize, Sustain) is an improvement activity focused on cleaning up and maintaining the order of a work space. The intent is to decrease waste, increase flow and improve quality and productivity by minimizing errors.

With an understanding of this basic set of tools, I had enough information to get started. We were ready to go.

Chapter TEN

Our First Value Stream Analysis – the Revenue Cycle

Our Black Belt consultants told me that for a complete transformation, we would start with an Enterprise Map. That would be the tool for identifying our value streams and prioritizing the order in which they would be transformed. But in our case, we had already identified the one with which we would start – the revenue cycle. That being the case, we were ready for the Value Stream Analysis. The Enterprise Map would come later, should we decide to fully roll out Lean.

The first thing Lana and I did was develop a charter for the VSA team. A charter is a very important place to start for at least a couple of reasons. First, the charter requires the executive sponsor to clearly state the objectives of the project, and indicate any constraints on what the team can do; for example, any budgetary limitations. It is very important that a team knows, going in, what it has the authority to do, and the limits on its authority. Teams can understand and respect these limitations if they are known up front, but there is nothing worse on morale and no greater momentum-killer than to have a team come back with recommendations that cannot be accepted because there was inadequate clarity around its limitations. Second, a charter gives the team organizational sanction, and the associated empowerment and authority to act within its charter.

We made the objectives very clear, and very focused:

Project Objectives: improve revenue cycle processes to reduce A/R days from 65 to 55, and to increase cash from 97 to 125 days.

We kept the constraints simple:

Constraints: any investment in people or equipment must have a payback period of less than 12 months.

A charter also identifies the executive sponsor, the team leader, team members, and supporting Black Belts. In this case, following Paul's sage advice, I chose to be the executive sponsor. As such my responsibility was to be an advisor and one who would support the team by eliminating organizational barriers that might impede its progress. I figured with me as the executive sponsor we were stacking the deck for success. If I couldn't remove organizational obstacles, who could? In addition, Paul suggested that I should actually participate in the VSA in its entirety. While executive sponsors are not typically expected to participate in the whole event, but instead support the team by participating in a daily out brief, he indicated that it would be a great learning experience for me. My full participation would also demonstrate significant organizational commitment and support.

Lana acted in the role of team leader for the project. In that role she was responsible for participating in the VSA, and then owning the rapid improvement plan that would get us from the current state to the desired future state. Team members included representatives from each of the areas involved in the revenue cycle. Importantly, in addition to team members from scheduling, registration, health information management, patient accounting, and other traditional "revenue cycle" functions, the team included members from nursing, care management, and IT as well since those functions are crucial to optimizing the revenue cycle. As Paul said, when determining who needs to be at the table, err on the side of inclusion rather than exclusion. While the size of the group may sometimes be a little unwieldy, the dividends, including commitment and achieving a critical mass, are well worth the effort.

We scheduled the event for three full days, 0800 – 1700. I wondered what the impact would be on the organization, having this key group of people out of their workplace for that long. Paul assured me that it was worth the pain, and again I deferred to his experience. I remembered that this was one of the things he told me about the very first time that we met. Turns out he was right on the money again. While it *is* tough to get people out of their workplace for three days, the act of immersing the team in a focused event really enables them to understand the process and map out a strategy for improving it. Get in and get out, rather than having an extended project that lasts weeks or months, meeting for an hour or two here and there. That is just not a very efficient process. A VSA on the other hand is amazingly efficient, as I learned during that first event.

Like everyone else on the team, I showed up not knowing exactly what to expect. I wondered whether it was going to be like classroom training, with our Black Belts basically lecturing us and telling us what to do to improve the process. That would have been very boring and quite unfruitful. But I had heard that VSAs are much more interactive than that, and they are. We did do a little training initially, on what the process would entail, and on the ground rules. The ground rules were intended to help make the event "safe," where people could openly share and discuss a wide variety of ideas. While the ground rules probably do need to be stated, the truth is that whether or not it is a "safe" environment depends more on how the leaders behave than on what the ground rules say. If a team member takes a risk by tentatively offering an idea, and it is met with criticism, they are not likely to take that risk again. Not that all ideas are good ones, but what leaders should do is encourage open dialogue and objective evaluation. There are various team brainstorming and problem solving tools, and when led by a skilled facilitator, these encourage the open generation of ideas and also provide a non-threatening process for identifying the best.

After the initial bit of training, we immediately got right into the process. First we had to identify where the process began and where it ended. That seemed obvious to me, at least until our black belt had us do a little exercise. He asked us to imagine that we were going to eat a steak. Then he told us to write down the steps in that process. A little mundane, I thought. You pick up your knife and fork, cut a piece of steak, put it in your mouth, chew it up, then you swallow it.

It was interesting for me to discover that everybody didn't see it that way. Lana, being more focused on detail, started with getting the steak out of the refrigerator. She said you couldn't eat the steak until you cooked the steak. Our procurement guy said well, you can't get a steak out of the refrigerator unless you put one in there. He started his process at the store. Of course, from there the team had a little fun and said 'well, you can't buy a steak from the store unless a farmer raises a steer . . . and you can't raise a steer unless you have some hay to feed it' . . . etc, etc. So for the purpose of this event, we decided the process began with the initial contact from a physician's office, and ended with receipt and posting of final payment.

Over the next 2½ days, we went through the rest of the steps of the process. We developed a current-state map, which captured the current process and various metrics for each step of the process; we developed an ideal state, that is, what we would do if we could start with unlimited funds and a blank sheet of paper; we captured the guiding principles that we employed in our ideal state map; then we utilized the guiding principles to the greatest extent possible in developing what we thought was a realistically achievable future state. Lastly, we developed a rapid improvement plan, which is the roadmap for getting from the current state to the future state.

One of the biggest eye openers to me was the waste walk. To begin the waste walk, the team developed a high level flow chart. Its purpose was to guide us through the process. Here is the flow chart we developed:

Then we took this map of sorts, and "went to the Gemba." The word

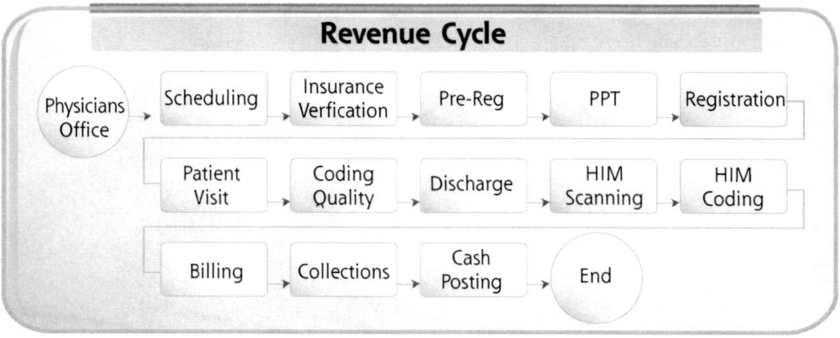

"Gemba" is Japanese and basically means "the actual place." The idea is that if the team really wants to know what is going on with the process, they have to actually go to where it is happening. So we took our map, went out to where the work was actually being done, and actually walked through the process. At each step of the way we talked to the people actually doing the work. We started with a fixed set of questions that we asked everyone, and then we delved deeper as appropriate. We started with this fixed set of questions:

1. Please describe your process: tell us what you do?
2. What is the trigger that initiates you performing your process?
3. First Time Quality (FTQ): What percentage of time do you estimate you have everything you need to do your job the first time?
4. What are some common problems you run into?
5. What are some opportunities for improving your process? That is, what would make it easier for you to do your job?

Paraphrasing the inimitable words of Yogi Berra: "You can see a lot just by looking." Truer words were never spoken. We were amazed at what we learned just by walking through and observing the process. It was also amazing how open the people were when they realized that we were not there to criticize them, but that we really did want to understand what they did, including the challenges they faced every day.

"You can see a lot just by looking." — Yogi Berra

As an example, just take the first step of the process—scheduling. This was already on my list of processes to improve since I found out that we intentionally left slots open so that we could accommodate urgent add-ons. But we found that that was just the tip of the iceberg.

Scheduling should be pretty simple process: a scheduler should receive a call from a physician's office to schedule a patient. The scheduler should ask what procedure or test needs to be scheduled, pull up the schedule, slot the patient, and move on to the next call. However, when we talked to Lisa one of our more experienced schedulers, we found out it wasn't quite that simple. First, we had two separate systems we used for scheduling, depending on what tests were required. That didn't make a bit of sense to me, and clearly complicated the scheduler's job. Lisa and every other scheduler had to know both systems. Ok, no biggie; so they learned two systems. Problem was, the two systems didn't talk to each other, so if the patient needed a CT for example, and also needed lab work, Lisa had to navigate between two separate scheduling programs to find appropriate times. She didn't have two computer screens, so it was back and forth between one software package and the other until she could find two slots that worked for the patient.

But even that was a manageable problem. The problem with "add-ons," however, was not so manageable. Add-ons occurred when a physician needed to get a patient in stat, and there were no slots in the schedule. I knew from prior experience that although there were no apparent slots in the schedule, some were vacant placeholders intended to accommodate these add-ons. I asked Lisa about it.

"Oh, that's just for CTs," she said. "But that is creating more of a problem than it is solving."

Somehow, I wasn't surprised. "How so?" I asked.

"The main problem is that not all of the schedulers use these 'placeholder slots' consistently, and worse yet, not all of the schedulers know how to tell which are actual cases and which are placeholders. So most of the slots never get filled anyway!" Lisa was clearly as frustrated as I was about it, and I reminded myself, again, that she was doing the best she could in a system not of her own making.

Lisa told us that whenever the need for an add-on occurred, she had to contact the clinical area and see if they could squeeze the patient in. Sometimes the clinical area would just allow her to double book, and then work the patient in. At that point, once the clinical area approved the add-on, you would think Lisa would have been able to add the patient in, but that too, would have been too simple! Schedulers did not have the authority to override the system, and had to call over a supervisor to do the override. So what should have been a very simple, straightforward process was a time waster for the physician's office that was trying to schedule the patient, our scheduling staff, and the clinical area.

We asked Lisa how often "add-ons" occurred. Was this an every once in a while anomaly, or did it happen a lot? She said it happened all the time, numerous times on a daily basis. We later collected data to better quantify the magnitude of the problem. Over the three days we collected data there were a total of 523 patients scheduled, of which nearly 20 percent were add-ons. Thirty or so add-ons a day! Talk about disrupting the system. No wonder we couldn't get the productivity in the scheduling area to where we wanted it. Not that the people weren't working their butts off, they were. But each add-on took at least three or four times as long to schedule as a "regular." Our schedulers were drowning out there, due to an ineffective and inefficient process for scheduling patients. But of course that didn't matter to our physician-customers, nor should it have. All they knew was it took way too long to schedule their patients.

We later learned that add-ons not only complicated the scheduling process itself, but there were also significant downstream effects. Take the impact on coding as an example. After the patient has been discharged, the HIM team pulls up the patient's record and codes the account for appropriate billing. They put a 'hold' on accounts that have some sort of problem, like missing orders, progress notes, incorrect disposition, etc. The coder we talked to during the waste walk showed us that there were currently 473 charts on hold due to missing information. Of those 473 charts, 378 – nearly 80 percent of them - had missing orders. And of those 378 with missing orders, we later discovered that a full 90 percent were from the add-on cases! So the add-on process created problems from the start, and these cascaded through the process. Incredible!

We had amazing discoveries in patient accounting as well. Anne, the supervisor, was extremely frustrated because less than 50 percent of our claims dropped cleanly the first time through. That required significant rework on the part of her team, but also meant we were holding bills and increasing our A/R days. Anne saw the data on a daily basis, including this summary from a typical day in the life of patient accounting:

Payor	# Claims	Claim Amount
Medicare Inpatient	62	$1,148,710
Medicare Outpatient	314	$819,719
Medicaid Inpatient	13	$247,573
Medicaid Outpatient	22	$39,612
Commercial Inpatient	27	$630,442
Commercial Outpatient	386	$781,511
Total Inpatient	102	$2,026,725
Total Outpatient	722	$1,640,842
Total Claims	824	$3,667,567

Of those 824 claims, only 327 were valid, for a total of $1,077,036 in clean claims. That left 497, or just over 60%, with errors. So we were holding $2,590,531 in claims. What's worse is that of the 497 "edits," i.e., what billers call errors, about half had to be sent back to HIM for resolution; and often HIM had to reach out further to the clinical areas. This added numerous days to the receivable.

Worse yet, of the half that could be corrected by the billers, the majority of those had already been reviewed and scrubbed before they got to billing. We were doing it twice! We discovered that our core HIS system does some editing on its own, so it was flagging bills, which were then reviewed and approved (no corrections required) by the clinical areas. Then these same edits were caught by our scrubber, and were then reviewed and approved (no corrections required) by our billing office! So we were scrubbing and rescrubbing bills that never had errors in the first place! Amazing!!!

The scheduling and billing challenges were just some of the many opportunities we discovered in those three short days. Altogether, the team identified 43—yes, forty-three—opportunities for improving the performance of the revenue cycle. Here are some of the other opportunities we identified:

Insurance Verification

- Incorrect patient insurance information not matching eligibility/verification software

  20 to 25 percent of patients require phone calls, averaging two calls each at 20 to 30 minutes

HIM Coding

- Missing orders, progress notes, dictated op notes

    of 480 bill holds, 78 percent had order problems

- Discharge disposition not correct

Collections

- A multitude of denials due to incorrect subscriber ID and missing authorizations

    Follow-up was overwhelmed and never touched accounts under $1,000.00

We were overwhelmed by the number of challenges our people were dealing with on a day to day basis. In addition, most of the issues had a significant financial impact. Our people were doing the best they could in a system not of their own making. As Deming would have said "This is a management problem. Management owns the system." We needed to make it easier for our team to do the job we were asking them to do.

We prioritized the opportunities and captured them on our "Rapid Improvement Plan," which became our roadmap for moving from this ineffective current state to a new and improved future state. For some opportunities, the solution was immediately apparent, like where we found an error in the decision logic for our follow-up software program. These we captured as "Just Do Its" on our rapid improvement plan. In other cases, the solution was not immediately apparent. For these we either scheduled a "Rapid Improvement Event" to further study the problem and implement solutions; or we identified it as a "project" which would require additional data collection and analysis to determine the appropriate solution.

Suffice it to say that this first VSA was the most enlightening three days I had spent at Healing University Medical Center. The knowledge we gained about the current state of the revenue cycle process was nothing short of astounding. It yielded fruit beyond my wildest expectations.

What really surprised me, though, was the cultural impact. The energy, the excitement, the esprit de corps, and the shared commitment that developed among the team members was phenomenal. Empowering the team, engaging their minds, and bringing them in as partners was a very powerful cultural transformation approach. I saw what

Paul meant. It was about the process—we had identified substantial opportunities for improvement. But it was also about the people. It was about the people improving *their* process to improve operational performance.

VSAs are unlike anything else I had ever been a part of. I learned that they are not at all lecture-based, but instead very, very active and interactive. Participants engage in multiple activities, including walking the process; standing at the wall arranging and rearranging note cards that represent process steps; doing affinity diagrams to identify waste and organize opportunities for improvement; and other very active and engaged tasks. There is more energy and excitement generated during a VSA than any other type of event I have witnessed. I think this is mainly because of the "aha" moments team members have as they really take the time to understand the process; the interaction with peers throughout the process; and the opportunity to actually identify solutions and plan for their implementation. In addition to being a great problem solving event, a VSA is both intellectually and socially stimulating. It is about the process; but it is also about the people, strengthening relationships and connecting people from across the organization, fostering a true team spirit and literally transforming the culture of the organization.

The event ended with a final round robin during which people had the opportunity to share final thoughts. I was amazed that a number of people actually thanked Lana and me for allowing them to participate. They spent three days of *their* time engaged in a very draining process, identifying opportunities for improving our organization. We should be thanking them. Instead, they were sincerely grateful for being asked to participate. I recalled a lesson Paul shared with me, which I had now seen for myself: *the act of inviting team members to the table, and empowering them to analyze and improve their own processes, stimulates ownership, motivation, and commitment*. So along with designing a new and improved process that would drive operational performance, the Lean event was, as Paul said, a cultural transformation tool. Lean *is* about the people *and* the process! And now the people were pumped up about their ability to actually improve *their* process!

Chapter ELEVEN

Implementing our Rapid Improvement Plan

"Yes, I'll bet the team is excited," said Paul as we debriefed the VSA. "That is a very typical experience. They get in there and see all the opportunities, and begin to have some hope that, after all these years, the process will finally be improved. The VSA was the fun and easy part. Now the work begins. As the executive sponsor, you need to ensure follow-through. The biggest challenge facing any Lean implementation is following through on the action plan. There is a real risk that you and the team will walk away from the VSA and get caught up in the day to day grind. As you said, you are good at fire fighting, doing what is important and urgent. Implementing the action plan you developed during the VSA will be important, but not urgent. You will have to be very disciplined and intentional to bring the plan to fruition."

"Great," I said wryly. "I thought the hard part was behind us! So, what now?" I asked Paul.

"Well," he said, "I assume you put together a Rapid Improvement Plan?"

We did, and I shared it with him (see next page).

Paul asked me to remind him who the team leader was, and I told him it was Lana Davis, our CFO. "Which of you is going to own the plan?" Paul asked.

Lana and I had already agreed that as team leader, she would own the plan. But I was still not totally comfortable with that. I thought that perhaps I should, since Lana already had a full time job. I just wasn't sure how she was going to do that and also do her real job—managing the revenue cycle. I shared my concerns with Paul.

Paul said he understood my concerns, but asked "What do you consider Lana's 'real job' to be?"

Rapid Improvement Plan

Healing University Revenue Cycle

RIE	Project	Just Do It	Description	Who	Plan Dates Start	Plan Dates Finish	Comments
X			Redesign scheduling process	Lana	4/1	6/1	
X			Redesign insurance verification process	Pam	4/1	6/1	In progress
X			Registration process coordinator	Brian	4/1	6/1	Registration, ER Nursing, Entry Depts.
X			Chart assembly start at point of entry	Cindy	4/1	6/1	Registration, ER Nursing, Entry Depts.
X			Common nursing database	Laura	4/1	6/1	Nursing from all entry areas
		X	Develop D/C Checklist	Anne & Monica	4/1	6/1	Nursing Unit Secretaries
	X		Review scrubber 'edits' and eliminate as appropriate	John	4/1	6/1	
X			Outpnt. order process & same day charts to HIM, Inpatient chart to HIM faster after D/C	Anne & Monica	4/1	6/1	
X			Develop tools for Q Review/Abstraction	Nancy	4/1	6/1	Quality & Care Mgmt.
		X	Leadership evaluation on revenue accountability/ tracking	Shannon	4/1	6/30	Org. Excel. Team, Chart VSA Team
X			Point of care scanning	Paul & Doug	4/1	6/30	Evaluate cost & available capital
		X	Standardize thinned chart and unidentified documents processes	Anne & Monica	4/1	6/1	Nursing and HIM
		X	Educate: all documents with patient at all times: - Explain big picture - Unidentified documents	Ben	4/1	6/1	Revenue Cycle Team
	X		Rationalize chart paper content, nursing floor process/workflow analysis	Glenn, Facilitator & Team	4/1	6/1	TBD & Laura/Lisa

I was about to talk about her responsibilities as CFO, but realized that Paul was being Socratic again. Figuring I was in for another lesson, I encouraged him to go on.

"One of the things I picked up along the way is a concept called the 'dual atom of work.' It's a very simple, but powerful idea: there are two parts to everyone's 'real job': 1. Doing the job. 2. Improving how the job is done."

That's a keeper, I thought to myself, and wrote it down:

The Dual Atom of Work: There are two parts to everyone's job:

- Doing the job.
- Improving how the job is done.

Paul's point was that improving the revenue cycle was part of Lana's "real job," not just something added to it. This concept was the only way that continual improvement would become a part of our culture. Every employee had to see improving their own processes as an integral part of their job.

"That makes sense," I said. "But it doesn't solve the problem of Lana having too much on her plate."

"Why does she have too much on her plate?" Paul asked.

"Because the revenue cycle processes are so broken that she is continually putting out fires and doing work-a-rounds to get the job done," I countered. "She and her team are working themselves to death because of the broken processes. I don't know how any of them could possibly take on anything else at this point. I know we need to do it, I just don't see how we are going to."

"What if the revenue cycle was functioning well?" Paul prodded. "Would people have time then?"

Of course they would, I thought to myself; with time to spare. If we could fix all our broken systems I'm sure we could do much better than we are now, and probably with fewer people. "But how do we achieve that?" I asked.

"Imagine that you and several members of your team are out in a boat, just having a good time. Suddenly you run into something that puts a three inch hole in the hull. The sump pump is overwhelmed and cannot nearly keep up. In fact, you find that it takes every one of you to bail, in order to keep your boat afloat."

I didn't have to try hard to imagine that! It seemed like that is what we were all doing at Healing U on a daily basis—bailing just to stay afloat.

"Your boat is well equipped, and you actually have a kit and the expertise to patch it. Kind of like your rev cycle team, when you think about it. You now have a plan for improving it, which you just acknowledged would both improve the process and free up people to do other work. So what are you going to do? You obviously can't continue to bail forever and not get anywhere. You have no choice but to fix the boat. What that means, unfortunately, is that those continuing to bail will initially have to work even harder so someone can go fix the boat. Same with your revenue cycle, and any other broken process. The truth of the matter is that people are going to actually have to work harder, before it gets easier. There's just no way around it."

Upon reflection I had to agree—there was just no way around the logic. Certainly we could authorize overtime, and perhaps bring in temporary help, but at the end of the day we were going to have to figure out how to get someone away from bailing and onto fixing the leak. Simply put, Lana was going to have to figure out a way to make the time to lead this improvement process so that she could ultimately have time to devote to more strategic issues.

"OK Paul, I see your point. So what does she need to do?"

"Well, as I was saying, before you rudely interrupted me (Paul kidded me sometimes—I really appreciated that he let me patiently interrupt his train of thought with my incessant questions, but every now and then he couldn't help but tease me about it) as owner of the rapid improvement plan, Lana should be responsible for the execution of the improvement activities. She is the 'boots on the ground,' and the day to day leader of the improvement initiative. She needs to ensure a consistent drumbeat of follow-up and accomplishment on the project.

In retrospect, this all made sense and reconfirmed what Paul and I had discussed before I started the rev cycle project. The performance of the revenue cycle was Lana's responsibility, so it made all the sense in the world that she should also lead efforts to improve it.

And lest I forget my own role as executive sponsor, Paul was quick to remind me: "Your role is equally important. As executive sponsor, you need to very visibly and very proactively ensure that the team maintains its energy and focus. Your people are now pumped up and excited about the work they have done, and the vision they have established for how the revenue cycle, and their jobs, could be so much better. The last thing you want to do is dash their hopes and their dreams by not ensuring successful execution. Should you not follow through, it will be very difficult for them to trust that any future projects will yield any better results. Remember that is why we wanted to pick a project, and a leader, stacked for success."

"OK. So I have to maintain focus—a rallying cry if you will, provide support, and eliminate barriers to successful execution. Lana has to lead the day to day activities of execution, right?"

"Sounds like a plan," Paul said. "Let me know how it goes!"

The next day Lana and I met to figure out how to best move forward. We started with our road map, the Rapid Improvement Plan. We had identified fourteen opportunities. Of those, eight would be studied, developed, and implemented through RIEs; two would be projects; and there were four Just-Do-Its (JDIs).

"OK," Lana said, remind me what the difference in these three things is?"

It is an interesting role for me to be a teacher of this stuff, since I was really just a neophyte, but of course the best way to learn something is to teach it. I had taken a lot of notes and done additional study since my first sessions with our Black Belts, so I did feel I had a pretty good handle on the "whats," i.e., the tools, if not the "hows."

Teaching Lana was a good refresher. I first reminded her what the VSA was: an event to help us understand our current state, design a desired future state, and identify the actions required to get us there. It yielded the Rapid Improvement Plan that we were reviewing and figuring out how to execute.

We determined that four of the actions needed no additional analysis, no additional go/no go decisions, but just needed to be executed. We put those in the JDI column. I reminded us both that, just because it is a JDI, it doesn't mean that it is necessarily quick and immediate. It simply means we have made the decision to do it, we assigned it to someone or some team, and they do it.

We determined that two of the events required additional study and analysis, the type of analytic or statistical work that is best done by an engineer or other analytically-oriented person. Those we call "projects."

Finally, we determined that eight of the identified opportunities could best be implemented using the Rapid Improvement Event (aka Kaizen) approach. These, like the VSA, would be intensive, all day long, facilitated team events. Unlike the VSA, they would be action oriented, the objective being to implement as much of the improvement opportunity as possible.

A review of the plan indicated that we had multiple leads assigned for some elements. For example, during the VSA, Anne and Monica had been assigned joint responsibility for the JDI "Develop a discharge checklist." Since it often happens that when multiple people are responsible, no one is responsible, we decided to appoint Anne the lead, with Monica as her co-pilot. We did the same for all the other assignments, assigning one person as the clear lead.

Then we refined the schedule for the RIEs. I reminded Lana that these action-oriented events would require multiple team members, and given that many overlapped, we needed to stagger the schedule to allow people that needed to be there, to be there. And then there was the need to continue to attend to the responsibilities of "their real jobs," so we wanted to ensure adequate time to increase our probability of success.

Supported by the team's hard work during the VSA, Lana and I now had to enable the team to execute. To do that, we needed to stay engaged and ensure regular and steady focus, and the identification and elimination of barriers. We decided that we would have bi-weekly team meetings, which would include everyone that participated in the VSA. We scheduled these for Friday mornings, and allowed ourselves a two-hour time block. We intentionally scheduled them for Fridays based on Paul's advice. He suggested that scheduling follow-ups at the end of the week provided the team a more timely notice and the opportunity to get things done during the week leading up to the meeting. At this bi-weekly review, each person assigned responsibility for an action, whether that be a JDI, RIE, or project, would update the rest of the team on status, including identifying any barriers or obstacles to completion.

Finally, we input the schedule and integrated all the actions and responsible leads into a Gantt chart, ultimately yielding a twelve-week project. This would be our monitoring tool.

Chapter TWELVE

Our First Results

I was a bit anxious to catch up with Paul several weeks later. We had the revenue cycle project well underway, and had already made some very significant accomplishments that I wanted to share with him. The problem was, there were also some areas in which the accomplishments weren't so significant. Truth be told, stagnant is a much better descriptor.

But first Paul wanted to follow up on our last conversation, when we discussed the dual atom of work and the need for Lana to own the plan.

"How's that going?" he asked me.

"I think it's going pretty well," I offered. "Lana seems really engaged in the improvement activities, and most of the RIE teams seem energized and are making good progress. Of course, Lana is working even more hours than ever, but not being one to complain, she is mustering on."

As Paul and I had discussed in our prior conversation, when you have to stop the leak in a boat, people have to work even harder to bail and fix the leak. Lana definitely owned the plan, and was working long and hard to execute it.

"What types of challenges is she running into?" Paul inquired.

"From what I can tell, most of the teams are making decent progress. They seem like they are continuing to meet. Lana did tell me that sometimes people don't come to follow-up meetings, but the truth is, people get busy. There are very important things that just have to be done."

Paul interrupted me. "What do you mean 'from what you can tell'?" He sounded a bit stern when he asked the question. Not like the Paul I had spoken to on many occasions. "Don't you know?"

"Well, yeah, I think I do," I said a bit defensively. I told him about the Gantt chart Lana and I had put together, and that it included bi-weekly status update meetings for the team.

"Are you going to those?" he asked me.

"Well, not all of them," I muttered, realizing that I had not fully taken his advice on being an executive sponsor. I started to make a weak defense, telling him that I went to the first couple, and that with the Black Belts help and Lana's leadership, everything seemed to be going pretty well. I also wanted him to know that I let the team know I was here to remove any obstacles that they might run into.

But from his own experience, Paul knew this was a slippery slope. "Remember what your role is?" he asked.

Of course I did. As executive sponsor I needed to "very visibly and very proactively ensure that the team maintains its energy and focus."

"What do you think is the best way to do that?" he asked.

I knew where he was going, but I'm also a CEO and don't like to be lectured by anyone. Then again, I did reach out to him. His experience, age, and wisdom made me more inclined to listen and learn rather than be defensive. Plus, he had selflessly given me so much of his time, and his advice. And I couldn't argue with his results.

So I checked my ego and with an ever so slight air of humility, gave him the answer we both knew was correct: "I have to maintain focus—a rallying cry if you will, provide support, and eliminate barriers to successful execution. I can best do that by staying involved in regularly scheduled out-briefs with the team."

"Indeed," said Paul. "In addition, your participation sets the example and tells people 'this is important' and they need to be there. Spotty participation by leader or team members is a slippery slope that leads to even more absenteeism."

"Thanks coach," I retorted, with a bit of good natured sarcasm. I recommitted to full participation in the project.

Paul was right, of course, and the progress we made over the next several weeks confirmed it. Just my involvement in the meetings spoke volumes of the organization's commitment to the process. People showed up, and they did their homework. We identified and eliminated barriers. We improved the process. And I learned a valuable lesson:

Leaders must be visibly involved

After that, things seemed to progress more quickly. Success breeds success. Once team members saw that their ideas were actually being adopted, they got really excited about implementing them. After all, they were their ideas for how to make their jobs, and our hospital, better.

For example, take Lisa, the scheduler that we talked with on one of our walk-throughs. She had to schedule patients through two different systems, which meant navigating back and forth between two scheduling programs. It was a significant waste of her time, and more importantly, it was a waste of time for the physician's office that was trying to schedule the procedure. It was a relatively inexpensive solution to get her an additional terminal, but one that significantly improved her efficiency, physician satisfaction and Lisa's sense of control over her job and the ability to impact her workplace. As a bonus, giving her what she needed to best do her job was a huge morale builder.

And there was Anne, the supervisor in patient accounting, who was aware of many of the problems but didn't feel empowered to do anything about it. On Anne's recommendation we got a software vendor in there to eliminate the unnecessary edits; and we ensured that edits that occurred through the core HIS were not repeated in billing. These two improvements alone dropped our A/R days by three, improved our collections since we had fewer problems caused by late bills, and significantly improved productivity in the billing area since they were doing so much rework. It also made Anne and her team's jobs a lot easier and she truly appreciated that her voice was heard.

I was reminded of another lesson that Paul had shared with me. He said his team members were initially wary of doing Lean projects, but after a while they embraced them. When asked why, they said "because management listens to us." Giving employees what they need to do their jobs is very empowering, especially if it is in response to their own suggestions. Lisa and Anne both saw opportunities for improving the process, but had been stifled for so many years that they just hopelessly trudged on the treadmill of management's making. It was their suggestions, elicited in the Lean process, which led to the significant improvement.

And I just couldn't get over the fact that they thanked us for letting them participate! Not only should we have thanked them, we should have begged their pardon for asking them to work in a system fraught with rework and frustration at every step of the way. I could see that they were proud to have been part of something important, and perhaps proud to be part of Healing U. And that made me proud as well.

Our team members *thanked us* for letting them improve their processes!

As I was still learning then (as I'm still learning now!) I decided to apply one of the tools I had learned – the checklist. I wanted to review the fundamentals of transformation and see how well we had accomplished each:

- We need a stable system
- Say what you do and do what you say
- Education & Training
- Checklists
- Internal Audits
- Culture of Compliance

Stable System. Well, we didn't yet have a stable system, but we were getting close. Through the VSA and subsequent Rapid Improvement Events we had mapped out a plan, had implemented it, and were in the final stages of hard-wiring it. We were definitely on the right track. At that point I had learned enough to understand that the next five bullet points in the list are the means for achieving the stable system. So a stable system is really the aim itself, not a method for achieving the aim. Then, once the system is stable, we can begin the real work of transformation: standardizing best practice.

Say what you do and do what you say. We were getting there. We had documented our new policies and procedures, and were following them for the most part.

Education and Training. *Check*—sort of. We were doing it but needed to be doing even better. We had some areas that were a little slow to adopt the new procedures, and we needed to ensure that we had fully educated them on why we were making the change, and train them on the new procedure. I made a note to talk to Lana about some additional team member development.

Checklists. *Check*!

Internal Audits. *Check*. We implemented these immediately after installing the new process. It helped identify areas and people that needed additional training or coaching; and it sent the message that we were serious about holding the gains.

Culture of Compliance. Getting there. All the above helped. But changing a culture takes time.

The results we achieved in that first project were astounding. When it began we had an average days in A/R of about sixty-five. We began the project in May, and after just sixteen weeks we were down to fifty-three days, beating our project goal of fifty-five days. Cash improved to 110 days, short of our goal, but nonetheless a huge improvement from ninety-seven.

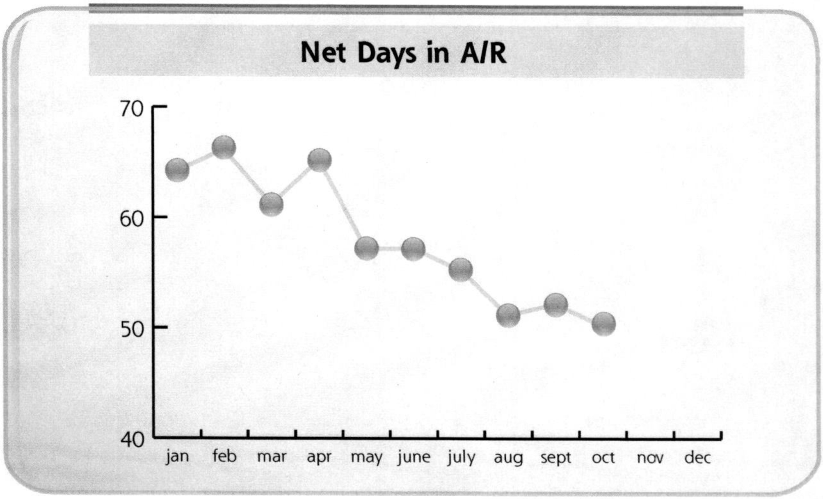

Paul was right, and after that project I had seen and experienced it for myself: It is about the people; and it is about the process. If we empower our people to improve the processes, they will. We have to give them the right structure, the right education, the right guidance and the right environment. Then we need to set them free!

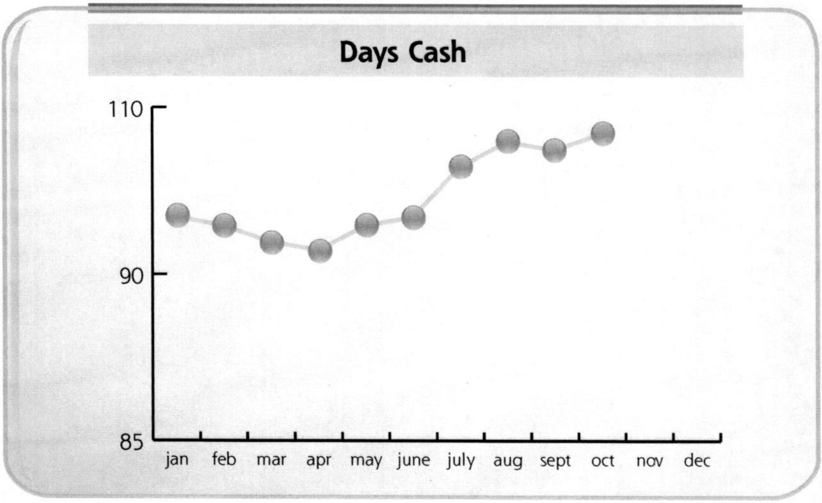

The revenue cycle project was the beginning of Healing U's turnaround. Success begat success and we were encouraged to expand our Lean transformation efforts beyond the scope of the revenue cycle.

Chapter THIRTEEN

Celebrate the Wins!

I was excited to talk to Paul that morning and tell him about the great results we had with the revenue cycle project! Healing U was on the right path! Paul greeted me with his normal warmth and graciousness, but over the course of our conversation I thought I detected an extra bit of excitement in his voice that morning. "Wow," I thought to myself, "He is really excited for me. What a true friend and mentor!"

It turned out he wasn't excited for me. Well, he was of course, but the excitement in his voice that morning came primarily from a different source. Paul had just discovered they had been named a finalist for the **Malcolm Baldrige National Quality Award**. "So much for my little accomplishment," I thought to myself. Then I caught myself and heartily congratulated him. "Wow—that is awesome," I said. "What a tribute to your efforts!"

Paul thanked me, but quickly shifted the credit to his team. I initially thought he was being humble, but he wasn't. Not in the traditional sense of the word anyway. He was not discounting his contribution to his system's success. Rather, he truly recognized the role that the many members of his team played in their transformation. As a wise man once told me "humility is knowing yourself as you truly are." That means knowing both your strengths *and* your limitations; your abilities as well as your inabilities; the role you play as well as the role others play. It is grounded in fearless and objective self-awareness. Using that definition of the word, Paul truly was humble. And he was still being a teacher and mentor. He was reinforcing the lessons I had recently learned about empowering my team and freeing them to achieve great results.

Humility is knowing yourself as you truly are

Paul also must have detected a hint of something in my voice. "Don't be discouraged," he said. "You are just now embarking on this journey, while we have been at it for years. Look, you have already reaped great fruit, and you are just getting warmed up!"

Of course, Paul was right. We were just getting started. I had already learned so much! We had already accomplished so much. What Paul was really doing was showing me the way, the end to which I could aspire. Not the Baldrige Award per se, but rather the organizational transformation and improvement that rises to the level of being chosen as a Baldrige finalist.

I again congratulated Paul, thanked him for once again, even unintentionally, showing me the way. Then I segued back to Healing U. "OK Paul," I said "what's next for us? I'm pumped! With Lana's good leadership, we have demonstrated that we can be successful in a non-clinical area. I'm raring to move into a clinical area; or better yet, engage in a total organizational transformation."

Having been there, Paul knew exactly where I was, and what I wanted to do. Having been there, he also knew that what I needed to do. They weren't the same.

"Lana and the team did a great job with the Rev Cycle project," he reflected back to me. "I think it's time to celebrate the win!"

"Yeah, we'll do that," I began. "That is important. We do want to thank the team for their efforts. But let's get on with the transformation!"

"Ah, but *that is* part of the transformation. Remember, it's about the process AND the people. You want to celebrate your team's success—recognize and thank them for their time, talents, and insights. That is part of the cultural transformation. Recognition is one of the single most powerful workplace motivators. The act of participating in the transformation, and achieving success, provides significant motivation. Recognizing the team's efforts will provide additional reinforcement of their improvement-focused actions and further amplify their motivation."

"But that is only part of the reason you want to celebrate. This was not just a success for the revenue cycle. It was a success for the organization. You want to use this opportunity to build support for continued transformation. Remember one of the lessons I learned along the way: don't push transformation into the organization. Rather, let leaders pull it in."

"Of course I remember," I said. "This is similar to the concept of not rolling out a new program, a new flavor of the month. I remember what you said: Don't announce a grand new program; don't roll out training to everyone at the start—do it just in time; start in an area in which you have a great chance for success. Build some excitement, and have other leaders 'pull' Lean into their areas."

"Exactly," Paul affirmed, no doubt thinking how great a student I was! I didn't bother to tell him I had forgotten that until I checked my notes. "You now have a success story under your belt. Celebrate! Thank the team. But celebrate the team's success organization-wide. This is a success not just for those team members, but for the whole Healing U community. Others will begin to get excited about how such transformation might benefit their areas, and their team members. Then you'll have the rest of the organization where you want it: hungry for transformation. After that we'll talk about next steps."

So celebrate we did. First, we had a little private celebration with everyone directly involved in the project. We bought pizza, and had a little bit of fun. Lana had the great idea to have a limbo contest. "Limbo contest?" I said, quite surprised. "Well, yeah," she smiled: "A/R days—how low can you go!"

"That's great," I said, still not quite comfortable with 'letting my hair down' in front of the team. But what the heck—it's ultimately all in the service of better patient care. I checked my formality at the door. We ate pizza, did the limbo, and had an altogether fun time in celebration of their success. Luckily no one sustained a back injury as the ED was on diversion yet again.

Then we featured the team and their success in a series of articles in our internal newsletter. We also contacted the local press, but it was hard getting them excited about reducing A/R days. "Let us know when you've got a human interest angle on it," my friend the editor advised. Yeah, I'll keep that in mind, I thought. It did have a human interest angle—the people part and the power of engagement and empowerment; but I must have been overemphasizing the process part. I made a mental note to be more balanced in my future communications about our Lean efforts.

We invited the team to make a presentation at our next quarterly off site. We gave them an hour on the agenda, and did it up right. Lots of encouragement and coaching beforehand, so that they would be well prepared and confident, primed for success; lights and music to introduce their presentation—like they sometimes do at the start of football or basketball games to generate energy, and excitement.

The team did a great job. They were proud of what they had accomplished, and sharing it with their peers and the leaders of the organization was a powerful affirmation of their success and strong motivator for future actions. The audience was pumped too. The team's excellent work and energetic presentation, enhanced by the pomp and circumstance of the event, yielded a contagious excitement and energy that permeated the room. The team closed to raucous applause. I wanted to start a chant: ***Healing* U! *Healing* U! *Healing* U!** But that would have been a bit overboard, maybe some other time.

At the end of the day, we got just the responses we wanted. The rev cycle team was appropriately acknowledged, and they felt truly appreciated for the work they had done. The rest of the organization was hungry for the same.

Importantly, they were not just hungry for improvement in their processes. Yes, it is about the process. But they were even more hungry for the empowerment to improve their processes—quite a distinction. They were hungry to be part of something exciting, to be part of a success, to have the affirmation of peers and superiors. It seemed to me that they were primed, and now was the time to capitalize on that success.

"It sure sounds like Healing U had quite a celebration," Paul said wistfully, when we chatted the next week. "What kind of reaction did you get?"

"Well, the team that was involved seemed really appreciative of the recognition. That limbo pizza party was some fun! I think they really enjoyed that."

"Yes," Paul said, chuckling. "I can imagine them doing the limbo with the boss. I'll bet that really meant something to them."

"I think it did," I said. "And in addition to the fun, I took a few minutes to sincerely thank them and let them know how much I appreciated their involvement and participation. Lana also thanked them heartily and sincerely. They seemed to appreciate our sincere thanks a lot."

"I'm sure they did. It never ceases to amaze me just how far sincere appreciation will go. And how about the rest of the organization? Sounds like they were fairly impressed by the team's presentation at the off site?"

"I think they were," I began. "The excitement seemed genuine. A number of other leaders throughout the organization approached various team members and Lana to congratulate them. They also seemed very interested in lean, and wanted Lana and the team to give them more detail about the transformation process, their perceptions of it, and what they really thought of it. The team responded enthusiastically to these queries and really delivered a powerful endorsement. A few of our leaders asked how they could get a Lean event in their area. I think the rest of the organization is ready to go."

"That's great!," said Paul. "Sounds like you have them right where you want them—pulling Lean into the organization rather than you pushing it on them."

Paul was exactly right, and our earlier discussions made a lot more sense now.

"They *are* pulling Lean into the organization!" I said to Paul. "How exciting!"

"Indeed," said Paul knowingly, having had the same rewarding experience himself. "So, what are you thinking about doing next?"

Chapter FOURTEEN

The Emergency Department — A Healing Pathway

I had given that some thought. I was thrilled with the success we'd had with the revenue cycle and was anxious to move forward. I wanted to do something with a little more meaning. No doubt, I was sure to receive plenty of pats on the back and congratulations from the board for our strides in becoming profitable. But, as I had discovered before, I didn't want this transition to be just about the numbers. I was really eager to make strides in our patient care. I wanted to be able to proudly tell my family and friends that I was the CEO of Healing University Hospital, rather than blushing when I said it. I wanted a hospital where I knew my loved ones would receive the best care possible. I wanted to be able to recommend Healing U to anyone in need of care.

I was fully convinced of the benefits of Lean implementation for improving processes and changing the culture. I wanted to roll it out across Healing University ASAP. And normally, that would have been my modus operandi: "damn the torpedoes; full speed ahead." However, I had been listening to Paul long enough to suspect that he would recommend a more metered approach. We hadn't ventured into a clinical area. It tried my patience immensely to do so, but I concluded that we should probably do a clinical area next, before we rolled out a complete organizational transformation process. I related my thoughts to Paul.

"I think that is a wise move on your part," he said approvingly. "I completely understand the excitement you are experiencing now, having seen the results. And the organization seems to be pulling for more. But although they may be ready, you may not be. I think you and your leadership team will be well served by taking another step before you start to run. At this point you have the momentum going your way and don't want to make a misstep. May I ask what clinical area you are thinking about?"

"Yes, and you won't be surprised. I'm thinking about the Emergency Department. It's our front door, where over 74 percent of our inpatients come from. Our beds are always full, and we are often on diversion. And you'll remember me telling you about my neighbor's poor experience. So this is a top priority for me. I know we've talked about it before, and one of the problems with improving the ED is getting patients into inpatient beds. So I want to include that challenge as part of the ED project." I clarified that for Paul, because based on my prior conversations with him it was clear he thought the ED was a tough clinical area to start with, particularly because one of the biggest challenges—the so-called 'back door' problem of getting patients out of the ED and into inpatient beds—fell outside the purview of the ED.

"Will," he said sincerely, "I think you have learned enough to appreciate the benefits and the challenges you are facing. You are clearly committed to the effort, and seem to have the support of your team. It is your hospital. If that is where your passion is right now I think you should go for it."

"I'm also thinking about delegating the Executive Sponsor role to our CNO, Don Baird," I offered.

"I remember him," said Paul. Isn't he one of the ones you were most impressed with—great memory, knows the industry—the out of the box thinker?"

"Yes, he is. I think he will do a good job," I said, without the benefit of hindsight. Unfortunately, I would later be proven wrong.

"Great," said Paul encouragingly. "It sounds like you are ready. Let me know how it goes."

As CEO I didn't need Paul's approval, but it was welcome nonetheless. I was a neophyte, and truth be told still a bit wary, so it was nice to have his encouragement. "You know I will," I replied.

"Oh, one other thing," added Paul. "It might also be time to add another tool to your kit."

"What's that?" I asked with curiosity.

"You might want to bring in a subject matter expert, or SME. That is, someone who is an expert in how Emergency Departments should run, with knowledge of current best practices."

"Best Practices?" I repeated. "I haven't heard you use that term before. I assume you mean the most effective and proven techniques for running an ED?"

"Exactly," affirmed Paul. It is sort of the equivalent of Evidence Based Medicine, but at the operational level. Someone who is well versed in the latest and greatest techniques will be able to bring value beyond what other members of your team possess. Your team members will come up with an enormous amount of improvement ideas. They may come up with some that have already been proven ineffective; or conversely they may not come up with some that are very effective but that they've never heard of. They only know what they know. Similarly, the Black Belts are experts in process improvement, but they don't necessarily have knowledge of industry Best Practices. SMEs can bring that Best Practice knowledge to the team."

I thanked Paul for his advice, and decided I would do just that. Of course it turned out to be the right move, so much so that we adopted this model going forward.

Later that day I approached Don with the idea of doing the next Lean event in the ED. He immediately agreed and expressed enthusiasm for it.

"That's what I've been saying all along," he said, as one whose sage advice had until now fallen on deaf ears.

"Great!" I said. We agreed that Don would be the executive sponsor. I was determined to step back and let him take the lead, with periodic updates on the team's progress. But I also decided that I wanted to participate in the Value Stream Analysis, since I was still learning and hadn't yet been part of a clinical project.

Don and I reviewed the responsibilities of an executive sponsor to ensure that he was clear about the role and my expectations. Then, as we did with the revenue cycle project and every project since then, we developed the charter for the team. Shawn Ferrell, the main campus ED director, would be the team leader. We also included representatives from our other two EDs, and representatives from radiology, the lab, IT, and the revenue cycle.

With regard to the objectives for the project, our average LOS was around six hours. It was totally unacceptable for our patients to have to wait that long to be cared for. Given the long waits, it was not surprising that our Left Without Being Seen rate (LWBS) was hovering around eight percent. So we chose improvement in these two key metrics as the goals for our project:

Project Objectives: improve patient flow through the ED to decrease LOS from six hours to four hours, and to reduce LWBS from eight percent to four percent.

The goal was modest by industry standards, but would no doubt be a challenge for us. We thought it an appropriate stretch goal for the first event. Like the revenue cycle, the emergency department VSA was a three-day event, morning to late afternoon. I knew there were a few grumbles about how people would get their "real work" done, being out for that long. But I had learned from Paul and my own experience with the rev cycle project that this was the most effective and efficient way to do improvement work.

This time I knew what to expect; and I anticipated with some excitement the waste walk and what we might learn. The event did not disappoint. Over the course of the event we were skillfully led through the steps of the process: the SIPOC, spaghetti diagrams, value stream map, etc. As with the revenue cycle, our greatest learnings came from actually walking the process, talking to the people, and asking them to identify the challenges they faced on a daily basis. I have come to believe that the waste walk is the single greatest tool in the Lean toolkit. Yes, you can see a lot just by looking!

What we saw were a multitude of improvement opportunities. The team captured these on note cards that we then organized using an affinity diagram:

Problems/Wastes Brainstorm

1) Signage

- Lack of ER focus on signs and sign quantities
- Parking lot full
- "Emergency" needs to stand out on signs
- ER sign in, registration, reception confusing
- Trees hiding signs

2) Perception of Downtime

- Five or six people standing or waiting
- Staff on Facebook

3) Waiting

- ER physician waits for hard copy of files
- Tech calls for patient and waits for ED to bring
- Two-thirds of films stored off-site
- Waiting for registration to get labels
- Waiting for radiology results

4) Undefined Processes

- Radiology ED priority
- Calling MD offices for lab results
- Multiple processes for radiology procedures
- Radiology tech in ER schedule/staffing
- Waiting for radiology results retrieval
- X-ray notification

5) Patient Tracking (bed board)

- Manual bed board

6) Documentation

- Organization of charts
- Finding charts to place results inside
- Too many radiology orders locations
- Patient tracking limited
- Waiting for US to enter orders
- Triage orders
- Triage protocols
- Have to go get charts from desk

7) Different Processes by Shifts

- "Request" print location and quantity
- ER physicians that order large number of CTs
- Delivery of specimens to lab on third shift
- Specimen pick-up not twenty-four/seven not named

8) Overproduction

- Reason for triplicate form at registration?
- Three copies of CT
- Radiology orders printing copies
- Tearing off lab labels and put in basket

9) Motion/Walking

- Patient walking to registration from triage
- Patient flow from ER to X-ray
- Walk from label machine to room
- Walking from lab basket to tube
- Techs walking from room to pick up registration
- Walking to call patient
- Walk from front room to back with specimen

10) Defects

- Redraws (One or two per shift)
- Urine specimen not properly labeled
- Lack of patient History (Radiology)
- Specimen not timed

11) Layout

- Triage room door too small
- Chairs at registration
- Radiology location—room size
- No room to maneuver patients
- Quantity of radiology rooms
- Glass doors vs. no doors

12) Prioritization (super stat)

- Priority Lab specimen
- Super Stat priority specimens—another phone call
- ER doctor did not know the color coded patient label (communication)

These came from the Eight Wastes typically associated with Value Streams. There were plenty of them.

Healing Pathways

As we reviewed this list of opportunities, one of our nurse team members, Mary June, made an observation that led to one of the greatest learnings we had along the way—the concept of *Healing Pathways*.

"Notice," she observed, "that most of the opportunities we have identified have to do with the process flow, impediments to the flow, work-a-rounds, errors, delays, etc. What's missing from this picture?"

"*Hmmmm*," I said. "I see where you are going with this. The patient!"

"Exactly! Think about what we just saw during the waste walk, from the patient's perspective."

During the waste walk, we had followed some patients through the process to observe the eight wastes in action. We saw one young lady who was obviously very embarrassed by her inadequate coverage as she moved from her bed to the bathroom in a split back gown. We saw an older gentleman who was on the verge of tears with stress and anxiety. Some patients waited in their beds for what must have to them seemed an eternity; and that after a hefty delay in the waiting room. We saw one of our nurses be very short and condescending with another patient. We observed how helpless many of our patients seemed. And no wonder. First of all they were sick. Second, they were in a strange place, with people and processes of which they had no knowledge or understanding.

When we thought about it that way—our very fragile patients turning to us for help—it was quite a humbling realization. And it certainly clarified our Mission: We are entrusted with the care of people who are facing some of the most difficult and lowest points of their lives. I again recalled how my mom was treated at Paul's hospital, and was determined that we would treat our patients just as well, and perhaps even better if possible.

We realized that the eight wastes didn't capture the entirety of the process. In observing our patients we realized the shortcomings of the Value Stream concept: they didn't focus enough on the patients' experience! One could have a perfectly flowing value stream, and yet not be providing a great, healing, patient experience!

As we thoughtfully discussed our observations in a spirit of open and honest inquiry, what occurred to us was that, in addition to the eight wastes associated with a Value Stream that impeded the flow of the process, there were also impediments that impeded a patient's healing progress. We started thinking out loud about what those were, and after much brainstorming and discussion came up with an initial list. We liked the way the Eight Wastes of a Value Stream could be remembered by a mnemonic using the first letter of each word, so we massaged our initial list and finalized what we have come to call the Eight Impediments to Healing. Here is what we came up with—using the mnemonic "SICKNESS":

The Eight Impediments to Healing

Stress & Anxiety	A common state of our patients created by the cause that brought them to us, uncertainty and fear about what may be wrong with them; and unfamiliarity with our setting
Inactivity & Waiting	Idle and unproductive time created when we cannot tend to our patients at a rate appropriate to their treatment
Coldness or Apathy	An aloofness or distancing from the patient by one of his or her caregivers
Knowledge Gap	The lack of information patients have about what is wrong with them, what is happening to them, and what is going to happen and when
Neglect	The absence of steady interaction and information sharing with the patient
Embarrassment	A negative patient experience caused by a lack of dignity in the treatment process
Submission & Helplessness	A state of learned helplessness exacerbated by information, power, and social status differentials
Statistic	Depersonalization of patients: for example "the chest pain in room thirteen;" five boarders, etc.

From that moment on, the transformation of Healing University Hospital was not just about our team members and our processes. It became about enhancing our Healing Pathways—the value streams through which our patients were treated and cared for. Not only did we identify wastes that impeded the process. We also identified impediments to healing. Our task became twofold: eliminate barriers to process flow; and eliminate impediments to patient healing.

Just as eliminating waste from value streams stimulates flow and throughput, so too does eliminating impediments to healing stimulate patient recovery. After that, we ensured that our rapid improvement plans contained actions aimed at both those purposes. In addition, we started thinking about how to more proactively stimulate healing through the patient process. Eliminating the impediments to healing was a great undertaking of monumental impact to our patient care delivery.

As our concept matured, we started to consider the opposites of the eight impediments. We called those the Eight Enablers of healing. Then we began to look for ways to promote the enablers of healing, rather than just eliminate the impediments. Here is what we came up with:

The Eight Impediments & the Eight Enablers

Impediment	Enabler
❍ Stress & Anxiety	Calm & Comfort
❍ Inactivity & Waiting	Progress
❍ Coldness or Apathy	Caring & Warmth
❍ Knowledge Gap	Abundant Communication & Understanding
❍ Neglect	Engagement
❍ Embarrassment	Dignity
❍ Submission & Helplessness	Respect & Empowerment
❍ Statistic	Special

The eight enablers became the core values of our system. They represented the ways we interacted with and cared for our patients.

As we considered these impediments to healing and their respective countermeasures, we came up with one last insight. Not much in terms of additional value to the improvement of our value streams, but significant in its implications and the message it sends. In Lean we focus on these value streams: processes through which products or services flow. The eight wastes are wastes typically found in value streams. We wanted to add consideration of the Eight Impediments when doing value stream analysis, rather than when products or services, were involved.

Mary June continued her star status by hitting on the idea of calling them "*Healing Pathways*" instead of *Value Streams* when patients are involved.

"Healing Pathways—WOW!" said the team, after it settled in for a few moments. Yes, exactly! Value streams through which patients flow.

Healing Pathways: Value Streams through which Patients Flow

We loved the idea. It excited us. And it sent a strong message about what was important. We wanted to understand more about what it meant, where it could lead us, what further insights and improvements to patient care it might yield. We continued to use the concept of Value Streams for support processes and the delivery of other products and services. But after that, whenever a patient was involved in the process, we called it a Healing Pathway. We chose to create this intentional division of processes into two different types: Value Streams and Healing Pathways. Healing Pathways are what our industry is about. They are the heart and soul of what we do. Healing Pathways, and not value steams, are why we are here.

After that, at Healing University Healthcare, Healing Pathways truly became our main focus. We even changed the name of the event from Value Stream Analysis to Healing Pathway Analysis anytime a patient was involved.

I was so excited that I was still absolutely bursting when I got home from work later that evening. I scooped Tyler off of the floor where he and Cinder were roughing it up a bit. I whirled him around in circles and carried him off to find Amy.

"What do you say I take you all out to dinner tonight? We had a huge revelation at work today and I feel like celebrating!"

Amy was thrilled to have me home at a decent hour and to be able to go out for a family dinner, which had not happened in a long time.

"So, what's this great revelation you've had, or is it top secret?" she teased me.

I told her all about the waste walk we had that day and the great revelation we had in doing so. She was especially interested in the Eight Impediments to Healing and the Enablers, being an RN at a nursing home herself.

Amy was as excited about the Healing Pathways concept as I was. "You know," she said, "I think this would be a great concept to share with the staff nurses and physicians at the nursing home. Would you mind if I used it there?"

I was doubly excited! Not only did I have Amy's enthusiastic seal of approval, but she also wanted to adopt the idea to improve the care of patients in her own health care setting. As it turned out, Amy and her nursing staff liked the Eight Impediments/Eight Enablers so much that they posted the list of them in the break room for everyone to see. She said it really helped to make everyone very conscientious when working with patients.

In retrospect, the concept of Healing Pathways was one of the accomplishments of which I am most proud, and which fundamentally changed our culture and our approach to patient care. When the team and I had this epiphany, I recognized it as something new and different to add to what I had already learned. Something I could share with Paul. Up until that point, he had been entirely the teacher, and I the student. But this, I thought, would be something he would consider a real contribution on my part. I could see him smiling to himself, thinking proudly of the impact he had on me. I couldn't wait and called him the very next day.

"Wow," says Paul, "You have taken this to another level." I smiled a huge smile and simply acknowledged it. "Yeah, we did!" For once, I was teaching him something. Of course I realized we couldn't have done it without him, and without our team members that actually had the keen insights. But we did it nonetheless. It was one of my prouder moments.

The next day we started with a Healing Impediments walk. It was similar to the waste walk, except that we were looking for the Eight Impediments to healing rather than the eight wastes. We decided that one of us should actually be a patient and experience the process from that perspective. I wanted to play the role of patient, but I figured that I would be recognized and wouldn't get the typical level of care. So we asked a relatively new member of Healing U, Dana from the IT department, if she would be interested in playing the role. She agreed enthusiastically. She played her role well, entering the ED with complaints of abdominal distress. She was able to truly experience the ED from a patient perspective. The rest of our team acted in the role of observers, just as we had the day before. We did our best not to betray that our primary focus was on Dana, and I don't believe that anyone in the ED knew what we were up to. We also actually talked to some of the patients, after carefully assessing whether it seemed welcome and appropriate to do so. Most were quite ready to talk with us. I think it may have even given them some comfort by distracting them from their ailments for a time.

The ED doc decided that Dana was fine but might benefit from a little more fiber in her diet. After she was discharged, we reconvened and debriefed our collective observations, and organized them under the eight impediments:

1) Stress and Anxiety

- Patient looked scared
- Lots of commotion in the ED
- Patient said she was afraid because she didn't know what was wrong with her

2) Inactivity and Waiting

- ED waiting room backed up with several patients
- Three patients waiting for a room upstairs

3) Coldness or Apathy

- Dr. Ames seemed distant when talking with patient in Room four

4) Knowledge Gap

- Patient was supposed to have an MRI but didn't know when it would happen
- Patient didn't know if free to go or still waiting for results

5) Neglect

- Patient in Room three for over an hour with no update or progress

6) Embarrassment

- Patient had to go to the bathroom but was uncomfortable doing so in hospital gown
- Patient uncomfortable with being in a bay that was open to "the world"

7) Submission & Helplessness

- Patient in Room three was afraid to ask for additional information and clarification when not understanding what was supposed to happen next

8) Statistic

- None observed.

It was quite enlightening to see it from the patient's perspective. We treated these opportunities for improvement with the same weight and importance as the eight wastes. We also decided to add patient satisfaction as one of the outcome metrics we would monitor, along with LWBS and LOS.

To conclude the Healing Pathway Analysis we developed the Rapid Improvement Plan, which identified a number of Just-do-its, Projects, and Rapid Improvement Events that would move us towards the desired future state. We developed a schedule for completing these, with appropriate responsibilities; and we scheduled bi-weekly follow ups to ensure we progressed as planned. We were all particularly excited to see what impact we would have on patient satisfaction. I handed the leadership baton to Don as Executive Sponsor, and looked forward to checking in with him in a couple weeks to see how it was going.

Chapter FIFTEEN

A Bump in the Road

"How's the Emergency Department project going?" asked Paul cheerfully when we checked in a couple weeks later.

"Pretty well," I replied, still excited about our development of the "Healing Pathway" and "Healing Pathway Analysis" concepts. But we were just a few weeks into it, and I hadn't seen the latest numbers on LWBS, ALOS or Patient Sat.

"How's Baird doing as executive sponsor? You sounded really impressed with him a couple weeks ago."

Wow, I thought to myself. I wonder how Paul knew to ask about that. I was starting to see some chinks in Don's armor.

"Yes, I was," I began. "Just weeks ago I considered him one of the two senior team members that would thrive in an environment of empowerment and process improvement. Now I'm not so sure. Remember I told you that he talked the talk about open communication and teamwork? Unfortunately he doesn't seem to walk the walk. During our staff meetings he has very little to contribute, but then I hear that he offers divergent opinions privately after the meeting and complains about the direction we are going. If that is in fact the case, he doesn't appear to be quite the team player I thought he was. In addition, his staff tells me he is very autocratic, and that although he solicits their opinions it seems to be for confirmation rather than dissent."

"Confirmation rather than dissent?" asked Paul.

"Sorry, that wasn't very clear. Apparently he presents a new idea or line of thinking, and asks the team what they think. I'm told they know he really doesn't want to know their thoughts, so they don't say anything. Then sometimes he asks again, and if someone ventures a differing viewpoint he reacts hostilely and belittles them for 'not knowing what they're talking about.' They believe that what he really wants is for them to agree with him. Apparently he spends most of their staff meeting regaling them with his past accomplishments and openly criticizing our current leadership team."

"That sounds a bit discouraging. How is his performance?" asked Paul.

"Hard to tell at this point. As you know the organization has been struggling, including nursing and the ED, which are under him. But he has reasonable explanations for why, and firm convictions on what we need to do going forward. I think the jury is still out on that. So far all I have observed directly is his relative lack of engagement in our staff meetings. I certainly hope I am wrong, but I am getting enough feedback about him from others that I am paying attention. Moving forward as planned will give me the opportunity to observe and coach him as needed. And maybe I'm wrong. What do you think?"

"How is he doing in his role as executive sponsor for the ED project?" Paul asked.

"I'll know later today," I told Paul. "We have our two-week follow up meeting later this afternoon. I should also have some preliminary results by then. I'll let you know how it goes."

Results came in just before my meeting with Don. Time to triage was amazing at less than six minutes. Left without being seen was down to 4.4 percent. But Length of Stay was unchanged at nearly six hours. Even more disappointing, patient satisfaction was languishing in the 45th percentile range. Hmm. I wondered why and looked forward to our discussion.

"Afternoon Don. I just got the preliminary numbers for the ED. Looks like you and the team have made great progress in time to triage and LWBS."

"Thanks. The team has done a great job" said Don with what may have been a hint of false humility.

"But ALOS doesn't seem to have moved. I'm curious about why that is. Patient satisfaction hasn't moved either. I sure thought we would have seen significant improvement there with the insights we gained from the Healing Pathway perspective. Based on the actions and dates in the Rapid Improvement Plan we put together I would have expected improvement in both those areas by now."

"Well," he said, "there's a lot going on. They just haven't progressed on schedule. But they are getting there."

"What's going on?" I asked sincerely, although I was beginning to wonder how engaged he was with the project and how much he really knew.

"Well, we've had some staffing problems and some of the docs don't want to change their practice habits," he offered tentatively. I was even less sure about his level of engagement, since these were the 'reasons' I had been hearing since I took this job.

I persisted, a little sternly "Where are we on the specific actions we identified in the Rapid Improvement Plan?"

"Well, I don't have that level of detail. I'll have to ask Shawn about that," he offered condescendingly. He was referring to Shawn Ferrell, the ED Manager and Team Leader for the project.

"Don – aren't you having regular meetings to review the status of the project? As executive sponsor you should have this 'level of detail,' as you call it. I don't consider it 'detail,' but the fairly high level status of the actions identified in the Rapid Improvement Plan."

"I'm letting Shawn handle that. He's doing a great job with it," said Don, again deflecting responsibility and further convincing me of his lack of engagement.

"Don, he's not doing a great job with it. ALOS hasn't moved. And I suspect it is not for lack of trying. Your role as Executive Sponsor is to help eliminate barriers and remove obstacles. Without your regular involvement and steady leadership this project will not be successful. Let me be clear about this: I expect your full and active participation and leadership as Executive Sponsor. Do we need to review what those responsibilities are?" I asked, with what most certainly must have been a tone of annoyance.

"No, I've got it," he stated flatly.

"Good. We will meet again next week, same time, same place, at which time I want an update on how things are going. Are we clear?"

"Crystal," he said with a hint of disdain.

Paul and I touched base later than evening, and I related the gist of my conversation with Baird. "He seems to deflect responsibility quite a bit," I observed to Paul. I'm sure it is clear to him that, as the executive sponsor, he is responsible for removing barriers and ensuring the success of the project, but he seems to blame others for what is not working. He doesn't seem to want to own the responsibility, although he certainly revels in having the authority.

"Interesting observation," Paul observed. "He sounds like a challenge."

"I'm beginning to think I made a mistake by making him the executive sponsor of this project. To be honest, I'm beginning to wonder whether he is even a fit for my team and this organization. But I also believe in giving everyone an opportunity to be successful. I have learned how important a leader's expectations are to getting the desired behavior from direct reports; and I also learned in social psychology how powerful the environment is in evoking behavior. So I am hopeful that if I continue to clearly articulate my expectations to him, and continue to change the organization's culture, he will respond appropriately."

I visualized Paul nodding his approval as he said "I respect the fact that you want to give him every opportunity to be successful. Based on the conversation we had earlier today, it sounds like you have a solid plan and will be there to assess and provide close oversight if needed. Staying with the coaching for success theme, in spite of his refusal, I recommend that you sit down with him again and review his responsibilities as Executive Sponsor. This will also provide a forum in which you can clearly re-emphasize the type of leadership behavior you expect."

Baird was still on my mind as I pulled into the driveway that Friday evening. It seemed like when I wasn't at work, which was most of the time, I was still thinking about it. Consequently, I had very little quality time to spend with Amy and my son Tyler, let alone any of my friends. I spent late nights reviewing graphs and processes and often laid awake thinking about work.

Amy was a real trooper about the whole thing. She knew, when I originally took the job, that it was going to mean a lot of evenings with just her and Tyler at dinner time while I worked late or had to attend various dinner functions. My friend, Greg, had been hounding me for a few weeks about coming to a poker game at his house that was set for this weekend and I had been putting him off using work and lack of family-time as an excuse.

Amy finally put her foot down and told me that I was going to go to that poker game whether I wanted to or not. "It's been too long since you've seen your friends and I think you really need a night away from your computer and work," she said to me. Well, since Amy was the boss in the family, I had no choice but to go.

I was glad I ended up going because it was the night full of fun and laughs that I had needed. It felt great to kick back and relax with my guy friends, just playing cards and joking with each other. I didn't tell Amy, but it may not have been exactly the work-free evening that she had intended for me to have. Greg had invited his brother Mike, aka Dr. Havens, to join us. Mike just happened to be one of our best docs in the Emergency Department. Naturally, the conversation strayed to the hospital, but not for too long. I was curious to know his opinion, from a doctor's point of view, on how the transformation was going so far. I knew we were getting a lot of push back from the doctors on the changes we had implemented so far and I wasn't quite sure why. They seemed like good changes to me, so why all the negativity?

"Will, I don't mean to criticize because I know you've got a lot on your plate, but I think you could benefit from getting the docs on board with you. I know I'm irritated with the changes being made and some of my colleagues are as well."

"I'm a little confused, Mike," I said, "I want you on board. All of you were invited to the Value Stream Analysis for the ED, but only one of you came, and for only a few minutes."

"Will, we have to cover the ED 24/7. We're all on rotating schedules, and they're fixed weeks in advance. We can't just not staff the ED and come to some Lean event, especially when it seems like we're an afterthought. You need to get with us before you plan these things."

"To be honest," I continued, "I really didn't think you'd want to participate anyway, considering that's not really in your job description."

"We're doctors, Will. We're used to being the experts on everything and we like to be the ones to come up with solutions to problems. I don't know why no one asked what we thought...we've just been having these new procedures pushed onto us. Some of these things seem silly so I'd like to know the ideas behind them."

"So, what you're saying," I summarized, "is that it would be nice if we got you involved up front and got your opinion on things."

"More than our opinions, really. I can't speak for anyone else, but I would like to be a partner rather than just a participant. When you are going to change processes and procedures that are affecting my work place, I would like to be somewhat responsible for them. I'd like to think some of it is my idea at least. If nothing else, it would be nice to at least help to shape the processes."

"Hmm," I admitted, "I hadn't really thought of it that way. You all really are the leaders in the ED, and you also see what is going on in there and no doubt have ideas on how to improve it. So it would be great to hear your opinions and ideas on improvement opportunities."

"That's it, Will. As docs we're all scientists at heart. We love looking at data and figuring out new things. If healthcare can be run better, our jobs will be easier. But we don't just want to be told what to do. We want to be partners, and we also want to see data that shows what is working and what isn't."

After that conversation with Mike, I felt pretty lighthearted. I focused the rest of the evening on just having a good time, but I knew come Monday I had some new things I needed to start planning which would include getting the docs more involved. Overall it was a very successful evening despite the fact that I lost $100 in cards.

After my conversations with Paul and Dr. Havens, I decided to meet with Don the next day to review the role of the Executive Sponsor and my expectations for his involvement and leadership. I relayed the gist of my conversation with Dr. Havens, and also suggested that Don needed to follow up to get the docs more involved. He assured me he understood his role and what was expected.

Unfortunately, when we met the next week it was clear that he either didn't understand his role, or wasn't willing to perform in it.

Don jumped right in. "The reason the ALOS isn't improving is because the staff isn't getting patients out of the ED and up to the floors," he began.

During the Value Stream Analysis, the team anticipated that this would be a challenge and they developed a solution for it. Consistent with practices beginning to emerge nationally, they decided that any ED patients that were to be moved to inpatient would be moved from the ED to the nursing units, and if a bed was not ready they would remain on their cot in the hallway until one was. We were skeptical as first, but the team, with the help of the Subject Matter Expert we brought in to participate in the project, presented us with current research findings that suggested this strategy actually resulted in better patient care, in additional to relieving the backup in the ED. So I asked Don about that.

"I told them we weren't going to do that," he said with authority.

"I don't understand," I said, after getting over my initial shock. We had already approved this part of the project, and to go back to the team and withdraw that approval would not be consistent with the culture we were trying to create. Don just didn't seem to be getting it. Moreover, the team did not see any other solution for solving the backup in the ED. "We already approved this."

"Well, we shouldn't have," he said, a bit too defiantly. "It's not my fault. The nursing staff just doesn't want to do it."

Not his fault. Right. Here he was again deflecting responsibility. This was not something I admired in senior leaders. Quite the contrary, I wondered what he was thinking.

"Have you gotten the docs involved?" I asked. "Dr. Havens said he would be very willing to work with the hospitalists and the nursing units to move that along."

"Look," he said, "If you don't like the way I'm doing it, maybe you should get somebody else to lead this effort. I've been in this business for 25 years and I know what I'm doing. This is the way we did it at Baptist, and it worked there. People just need to do what I'm telling them to do."

I ignored his veiled threat long enough to recall another observation I had recently made about Don. While I initially was impressed with the amount of ideas he had, I discovered that most of them were simply reflections of what he had done in previous jobs. It seemed that whatever way he learned to do something—even if it was twenty years ago and under completely different circumstances—was the way it should be done. Just like his last comment: "this is the way we did it at Baptist."

I realized that the truth of the matter was that he was not the "out-of-the-box" thinker I first thought he was. He was simply playing the same old tired tapes of what he first learned, over and over again. As confirmed by this current conversation, he was also not one to take responsibility for failures. As I thought about it, he had never once admitted to having made a mistake, always deflecting blame to someone else, or circumstances beyond his control. He certainly didn't get the idea of open communication and empowerment, as evidenced by his recent intervention in the ED project. It was clear that he was not going to change. His personality characteristics, as dysfunctional as they might be, were long ingrained. And finally, this latest outburst of total disdain and disrespect for his direct supervisor convinced me that having him on the team was not in our best interests.

"I'm afraid I agree Don," I said calmly, although I was quite distressed on the inside. It's never easy to let someone go, in spite of their poor performance and inappropriate behavior. But it is sometimes necessary. "I don't think this is going to work out. I'm going to have to let you go."

He seemed momentarily surprised, but quickly regained his composure. "Fine," he said, "Good luck doing this without me," as he stormed out of my office.

Things went much more smoothly after that. The truth of the matter is that, to be successful, you have to have the right people on the team to build the culture that you want. As the CEO, I have a primary responsibility to the organization, not to individuals. I do recognize the power of the environment and a leader's expectations in molding behavior, so I want to give every individual the opportunity to be successful. But sometimes, in spite of our best efforts, there just isn't a fit. In those cases it's better for everyone involved, even the person terminated, to move on.

Tim Wessel, my COO, volunteered to step in to the role of Executive Sponsor for the project. I think Tim was initially a bit of a skeptic about Lean. But he was also quite intelligent and swayed by objective data. The success of the revenue cycle project convinced him of the benefits that could be achieved, and he was eager to step in and help.

Tim's participation was most welcome to me, and significantly alleviated my concern over the potential impact of Baird leaving the organization. Tim was well respected by staff and physicians alike. He was also very results oriented and very committed to the Mission of our organization, and to the accomplishment of his personal responsibilities. I was confident that, having embraced Lean and volunteering to provide the leadership for this project, Tim would no doubt fully commit himself to it.

The ED turned out to be one of our biggest and most successful projects. It is also one of the most amenable to the application of

Lean flow analyses. We achieved great results in throughput, LWBS, and reduced hold times to get inpatients to the floor. Moreover, the morale of our staff and physician team had never been better. They were energized by the improvements they were able to make, and took well-deserved pride in their accomplishments.

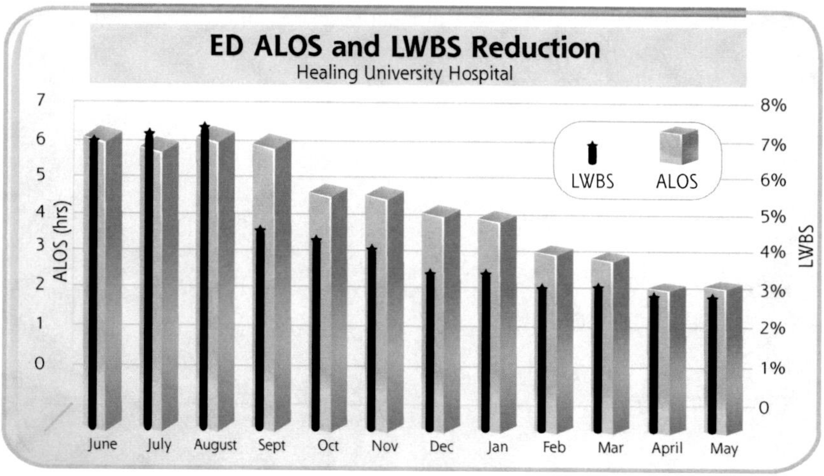

And our patients? We hit it out of the ballpark with them! The Healing Pathway concept really challenged us, and guided us, to see the ED experience from the patient's perspective. During the Healing Pathway Analysis we found many of the Eight Impediments to Healing; and we redesigned the ED and its Healing Pathway to maximize the Eight Enablers of patient healing.

Some improvements required adaptations to the physical structure of the ED itself. But by far the most significant improvements came from the change in our people. There was a palpable attitudinal shift as the true concept of seeing it from the patient's perspective took hold and became part of our culture. We began to share more information and communicate more frequently with our patients. We became much more mindful of the fact that they are people, not just "patients" and "diagnoses." That relatively minor change in perspective had monumental impact on how we engaged with them. It enabled us to be more caring, more empathic to their situation and their needs, more respectful, and to treat them with much greater dignity. And the response of the patients was overwhelmingly positive and appreciative, providing its own intrinsic rewards to the staff in an extremely positive cycle of mutual reinforcement.

Patient Satisfaction - Emergency Department

Metric	Baseline	Goal	Sep	Oct	Nov	Dec	Jan
Percentile	44	80	45	87	98	99	99

Chapter SIXTEEN

The Healing Way - Standardize Best Practices

Early one Saturday morning I was awakened to the sound of a giggling child, and if I wasn't mistaken, a giggling wife. "Alright, what's so funny, you two," I groggily asked?

"Daddy, you look really funny in this picture!" Tyler said as he squirmed into bed with me. Amy was right behind him holding the newspaper out to me.

"It's really a great article, honey, but what were they thinking using this picture? I mean, you look like a cross between a cowboy and a fireman...but not in a good way," she smirked. "I didn't know that was possible."

I had given an interview to the local paper about our Emergency Department turnaround and it was featured in the Metro section in today's paper. The picture they had used for the article had me in a tweed vest in the back of an Ambulance leaning against it somewhat seductively. We had a little fun in the photography shoot but I had no idea they would actually use one of my "less professional" pictures! I had to admit, it was a pretty funny picture.

"Ok, ok. Enough of the laughing. Is the article any good?"

"Oh, Will! The article is great! I knew you made some great changes in the ED but it's wonderful they did an article on it, for all the community to see. This is going to be great for Healing U's reputation!" She was absolutely beaming, like the proud wife she was. "Not to mention the improvement in patient care."

It actually was a great article, and extremely flattering—to me and to the team. The headline read "Empowered Team Members Transform Healing U's ER." The article included strong testimonials from our team members and from our patients. I had a feeling this article was going to make big strides in getting patients back to our ED (not that I was wishing medical emergencies upon anyone!). Our reputation had been sliding for a few years, and rightfully so, but with this turnaround things were getting back on track. The most gratifying thing for me was that the changes we made were not only great for business practices but they were also great for the patient. That was my goal. I was pleased that the ED transformation had gone so well, and I was energized to start the whole hospital's turnaround to make Healing U a hospital I was proud to call my own.

The rest of the day was filled with congratulatory phone calls from family and friends with a few lighthearted jabs at my photo. I was advised in no uncertain terms to not quit my hospital job to take up modeling.

With two successful projects under our belts, I was convinced that it was time to move forward at an organization-wide level. I was hoping Paul would agree. I was afraid he might think I was being a bit overenthusiastic about moving forward, and might think we weren't quite ready. But I saw what Lean and its associated cultural transformation could do for us. I was hopeful that it could help us turn the corner towards delivering better patient care—care like my mom got at Paul's hospital. Most importantly, I wanted our patients to have a safe experience. I wanted to never have so called never events—adverse patient events that are serious and largely avoidable. I wanted great patient care as evidenced by excellence on core measures and patient satisfaction. I wanted our physicians to be completely satisfied—no, more than that. To use Dr. Havens words, I wanted them to be proud partners of Healing U. I wanted the same for our team members. I wanted what Paul had: to be nationally renowned as one of the best. And if on top of all that we could make a three or four percent margin, life couldn't get any better!

"It sounds like you are ready," said Paul, a little to my surprise.

"We are?" I said, before I caught myself. "Uh, I mean—yeah we are!" And although I had a general idea on how I thought we should proceed, as always I wanted to benefit from Paul's experience. "How do you recommend we proceed?" I asked.

"The answer is simple," Paul said, "but unfortunately not easy."

Another 'Paulism!' I had to write that one down too:

The answer may be simple, but not easy!

Hmm. Simple, but not easy. "OK, I'll bite", I thought to myself. "What do we need to do?"

"Simply put, more of the same. As you said, you have two successful projects under your belt. Expand your efforts by empowering your people to help you transform Healing U," he said.

"What do you mean by transform?" I asked. I had learned the valuable lesson of empowerment through the revenue cycle and emergency department events. But so far we have mainly used the word "transformation" in the context of a cultural transformation.

Paul said, "the word transformation is used broadly in our industry to label a lot of different efforts. What I mean by it is this: empower your people to standardize best practices across the organization."

That seemed pretty important, so I wrote it down too:

Transformation means empowering your people to Standardize Best Practices across the organization.

As I thought about it, this was really the integration of two concepts that continued to recur in my conversations with Paul: Lean as a cultural transformation tool; and standardizing best practices. So what Paul was suggesting was engaging our full team in helping to standardize best practices across Healing U. As Paul had learned through the school of hard knocks, you don't transform the culture before you do process improvement. Whether you call it TQM, Lean, Lean Sigma, or Standardizing Best Practices, you transform the culture by empowering your people to improve their processes. Transformation is the act of empowering people, in an environment of open inquiry and learning, to collectively and synergistically work with their peers across a value stream to improve their own processes. I asked Paul, half-jokingly, whether this was the simple part or the not easy part.

"Well, it's both" he smiled, knowing that I was both kidding and serious. "The concept is simple. The execution can be fairly straightforward if done correctly and with the appropriate resources and support. What makes it difficult is maintaining focus, following through, and holding the gains. That is the part that is not so easy.

I was ready to get on with it, and nearly missed what Paul just said, and the importance of it. Paul must have noticed, and reiterated:

The challenge with any worthwhile transformation effort is maintaining focus, following through, and holding the gains.

I still wasn't 100% convinced. It seemed to me that the actual Value Stream or Healing Pathway Analyses, and all the associated improvement activities, were the most important.

"Those are critically important," Paul replied. "But in my experience that is the relatively easy part. During the actual improvement events people are very focused, very energized, even having fun! They come up with great ideas. But the real challenge occurs when the event is over, when they have to go back to doing their 'real jobs.' That is when the danger of not following through is the greatest. You need what some call a 'drumbeat' of follow up—that is, regular, consistent, steady review of a project or transformation effort until it comes to completion as evidenced by it becoming the new, hard-wired norm. Without the drumbeat of consistent and steady follow-up you will likely never achieve crystallized and hard-wired transformation. Worse yet, you will disappoint all those team members that participated in the Lean efforts with hopeful expectations that things would improve."

Paul was so ardent and passionate in his explanation that I was convinced he *did* think this was the hardest part of the transformation.

"How did you ensure that you hard-wired the gains?," I asked.

"Let me send you a figure to help you understand it," he said, and emailed me a diagram. I tweaked it a little bit to show "Healing Pathway Transformation" where Paul had put "Value Stream Transformation":

"Consider the organizational transformation as occurring at three distinct yet highly interdependent levels," he explained. There are different roles and responsibilities at each level, and each level can be depicted by the PDCA cycle which we have discussed on numerous occasions. The main point here is that, at each level, there is an ongoing Check—i.e., determining whether or not the desired results are being achieved—and an Act - i.e., eliminating any identified obstacles and ensuring follow-through and execution. Here is a brief summary of the activities and responsibilities of each level:

- **Enterprise Transformation** focuses on the healthcare services and enterprise-wide systems, while directing specific healing pathway and value stream transformations. The Enterprise Transformation must be led by the Chief Executive Officer and the Senior Leadership Team. It is their responsibility to direct and prioritize transformation efforts in alignment with the enterprise's strategic and operational priorities. The Enterprise Transformation will be guided by a Transformation Plan that will be developed by the Senior Leadership Team during the Transformation Summit.

- **Healing Pathway Transformation** focuses on hi-level processes that constitute the Healing Pathways (clinical processes) and Business Pathways (Value Streams). Healing Pathway Transformation must be led by the Senior Executive over the respective area. Transformations will be guided by a Healing Pathway Analysis and Rapid Improvement Plan that will be developed by the Executive and other key leaders during a Healing Pathway Analysis Event.

- **Process Transformation** focuses on the specific processes that combine to form the Healing and Business Pathways. Process Transformations must be led by the senior manager over the respective area. Process Transformations will be guided by action items developed by teams or individuals during improvement efforts including Rapid Improvement Events, Six Sigma projects, Five S's and others.

One of the lessons I thought I had learned from Paul was basically to "just do it." He had advised not rolling out a new program, not training everyone in the organization, not announcing a new program. But rather, training a vital few, just-in-time, then getting started. So I surmised that the next steps here would be to "just do it."

But Paul's experience had taught him otherwise. "Now that you have demand within the organization, the pull from within, the organization is ready to embrace a Lean-based transformation. So you don't have to be as concerned about protecting against a "flavor of the month" perception. What you do have to guard against now are false starts, and failing to deliver on your team's expectations. Success at this point requires some fairly detailed planning, including a roadmap of what you want to accomplish, in which areas, and how you will sustain the gains. I recommend you begin with a facilitated off site of your top thirty or so people. I call it a Transformation Summit.

"Do you mean a strategic planning session?" I asked.

"No, this is different. Strategic planning is necessary for the long term success of an organization. ***Transformation*** is the process of reinventing the way you do what you currently do. The purpose of the Transformation Summit is to prioritize those parts of the organization that need to be improved. This should be done at a fairly high level—a Value Streams or, to use your new terminology, a Healing Pathways level. Then you will develop a very integrated and fairly detailed plan for how you will accomplish The Transformation Process.

"So," I summarized to help clarify my thinking, "We want to identify the high-level processes—Value Streams and Healing Pathways—such as the Emergency Department, Surgical Services, Medical Imaging, Lab, In-Patient Care (Nursing), Revenue Cycle, Supply Chain, etc."

"Precisely," said Paul. "These will be developed as part of your enterprise map. The final list will be developed and prioritized with input from your top leaders at this off site. Then you will want to assign one of your execs the responsibility of leading and ensuring the transformation of that Value Stream or Healing Pathway. In other words, they will act in the role of Executive Sponsor, just like you did for the Revenue Cycle, and like Tim Wessel did for the Emergency Department."

"Sometimes," Paul continued, "it will be obvious who should be the executive sponsor. For example, in areas like the supply chain, revenue cycle, and human resources, where you have an individual with corporate-wide responsibility, the senior leader over that area is the likely candidate. In other cases, including some of the clinical areas like the ED or surgical areas, where there is no single corporate leader, you'll want to assign someone the responsibility of Executive Sponsor. It may be a temporary position, but it should be a full-time position at least until the new system is designed and implemented."

"Finally," Paul concluded, "over the course of the transformation effort you will likely want to establish matrix reporting relationships. The functional areas in each operating unit will have a 'solid-line' to the operating leader, and a 'dotted-line' to the Value Stream Executive Sponsor. Additionally, in those areas where applicable, a Physician Executive Sponsor should be assigned to work with the Value Stream Executive Sponsor in developing the standards for the value stream. Structurally, the organization may look like this for Healing U:

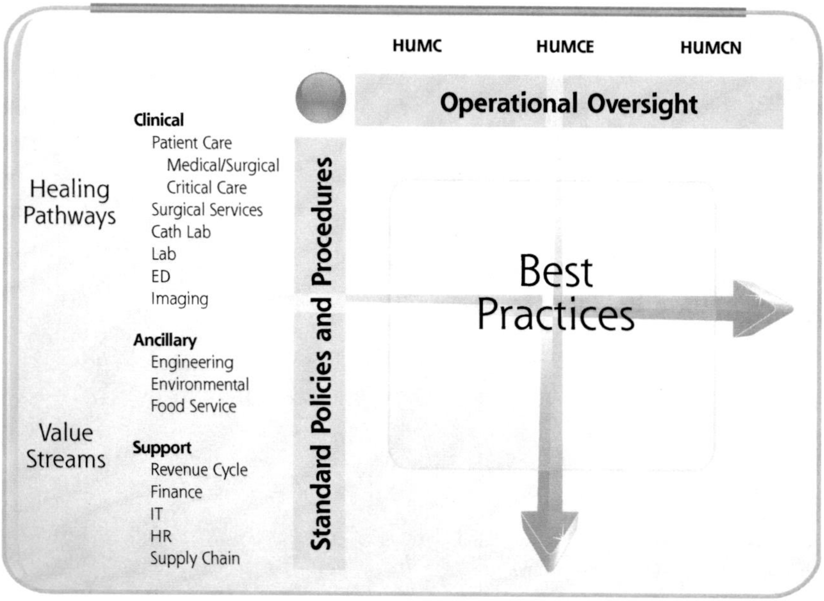

The drawing made a lot of sense to me. It clearly illustrated what Paul meant by high-level Healing Pathways and Value Streams—things like patient care, surgical services, engineering, and the revenue cycle. It also emphasized that Best Practices for each should be standardized across our system. This included the Main Campus (HUMC) and our two ambulatory Medical Centers—Healing University Medical Center East (HUMCE) and North (HUMCN). I could envision a separate team with responsibility for standardizing each of the high-level processes across all the sites. That is exactly what Paul had in mind.

"Under the leadership of the Value Stream Champion, and with the support of your Black Belts, each Value Stream will identify and plan to implement Best Practices, document them in policies and procedures, and oversee their full implementation," he said.

"That makes sense," I replied. "And like our rev cycle and ED projects, I suspect we will start each with a Value Stream or Healing Pathway Analysis as appropriate, and implement with a series of Rapid Improvement Events (RIEs), Projects, and Just-Do-Its. Correct?"

"You got it," Paul affirmed. "And in addition to including the operational leaders, and physicians as appropriate, you will also want to include your IT experts and appropriate Subject Matter Experts (SME) for each area."

I knew Paul was right-on. Bringing in our external SME for our ED project was a real value-add and enabled us to implement some improvements we would have never even considered, such as using a physician in triage.

The more we talked, the more I became concerned about the magnitude of the transformation effort. It would be imperative that representatives from each facility participate in the VSAs and RIEs. That would mean full-time involvement when events were held in their functional area. When events were not underway, less of their time would be needed, but it would still be critically important that they stay fully engaged. Plus, we were gearing up to move from our 'best of breed' strategy to a single core Health Information System. We're trying desperately to meet ARRA and hi-tech requirements, just like nearly everyone else, and that was going to be a huge undertaking in itself.

"Paul," I said, sharing my concerns with him, "my people are already going to be overwhelmed with our migration to a new IT system. I'm not sure we will have any additional bandwidth for transformation. Maybe we should delay our efforts until we have the new system in place."

"That is a huge undertaking," Paul acknowledged. "I have a couple thoughts about that that you may wish to consider. First, the reality is that there will always be 'something else' going on. Remember our discussion about being in a boat that requires everyone to bail, just to stay afloat? Someone had to nonetheless stop bailing and fix the leak, meaning everyone had to work even harder for a time. That's part of what you are getting yourself and your organization into by pursuing transformation. It is going to get harder before it gets easier. You want to go in with eyes wide open, and realize that you and the rest of your senior team must support this time commitment in order to enable the transformation's success."

I knew he was right, but it wasn't much consolation. "And your second thought?" I asked.

"My second thought is that you may have a once in a lifetime opportunity. Successful installation of your new core HIS will be complicated by your lack of standardized processes. Use the new core HIS as a forcing function to help you Standardize Best Practices across the organization before you install it. I think your timing couldn't be better. In the words of one of the Black Belts I have had the pleasure to work with: Obliterate before you automate."

That was a keeper, I thought, and wrote it down:

Obliterate before you automate
—Chuck DeLadurantey

And it was also an interesting idea. If we could pull it off, we could align all of our efforts and resources—team members, IT vendor, and SMEs alike—behind one major initiative: developing a solid framework for the Transformation and IT migration, and leading its implementation. I shared that observation with Paul.

"I agree completely," said Paul encouragingly. "I would envision that implementation of re-engineered processes and migration to the new IT system would not proceed until each of the Value Streams and Healing Pathways has been reviewed and standardized throughout the system. The re-engineered processes and HIS system could then be implemented at a pilot site, perhaps one of your ambulatory centers, and thereafter rolled out to your other ambulatory site and the main hospital. This approach would help ensure that any issues are resolved at the pilot facility, and maximize resources available to support implementation at follow-on sites. Remember the lesson 'do a little, learn a lot.' It applies here too!"

Could we really do both at once—transformation and migration to a new IT system? It was an exciting prospect, but also a bit overwhelming. "Slow down Paul," I said. "We just covered a heck of a lot of ground. I need a minute to process it."

He chuckled and said "sorry – I tend to get carried away sometimes. But remember that even a journey of a thousand miles begins with just one step. You'll do this the same way: one step at a time. Step 1: get your team together…."

With that bit of wisdom and encouragement from Paul, and confident that he would be there to provide advice and counsel as needed, I was ready to make the commitment.

I wondered how long it would take. I wanted it done yesterday, of course. Paul indicated that we would develop a very reliable and detailed timeline as part of the Plan of Objectives and Milestones (POAM) at the transformation summits, but for planning purposes he said we would probably need 18 – 24 months to completely transform all our value streams and install the new core HIS. Like usual, it turned out he was right on the money.

"One last thing," Paul offered. "And this is extremely important. Remember we just talked about how critical it is to ensure a steady drumbeat of follow-up at the organizational transformation level? It is the same at the Value Stream and Healing Pathway level. In order to sustain and hardwire improvements, you are going to need disciplined and steady follow up.

"At the system level, you may want a corporate internal audit function to provide ongoing system performance, progress, and compliance auditing. You may also want a system-wide corrective and preventive action system to provide appropriate tracking and feedback mechanisms. Your Black Belts can help you describe and document these in a corporate policy regarding internal audits, corrective action (CA), and change-management activities.

"You will also want to develop audit procedures as appropriate, for each Value Stream or Healing Pathway as part of the VSA or HPA. These might include an audit plan which identifies the key parts of

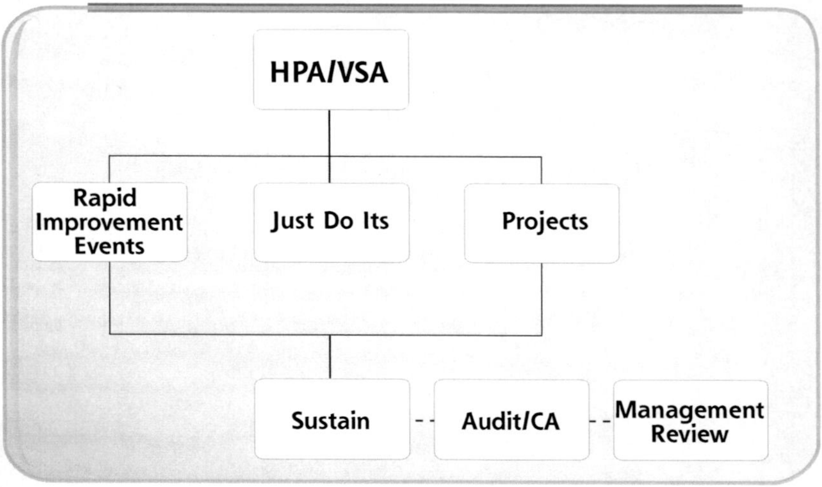

the process to be audited, the team member who will perform the audits, and the frequency at which they will occur. Sorry if I am beating this to death," Paul apologized, "but this truly is one of the most important lessons I have learned. Teams leave lean events pumped up and excited. Your leadership team will leave the Transformation Summit the same way. The challenge comes in following up on the actions developed during these planning activities."

That was certainly a lot to absorb in one conversation with Paul. But as I digested and thought about it, I realized that implementation of our new core HIS system really could serve a useful role—a forcing function, if you will—to drive us to timely transformation of our organization. It truly represented an opportunity to completely re-engineer and establish the Healing Way for all processes across the system. And it would help us hard-wire them, which Paul continued to highlight as the most challenging part of the transformation. In retrospect our timing couldn't have been better. The need to standardize processes for implementation of the new core HIS system served as the catalyst, and also presented a once-in-a-lifetime opportunity to develop, implement, and standardize best practices.

Chapter SEVENTEEN

The Transformation Summit

I took Paul's advice and brought in our Lean consultants to help plan and conduct the transformation summit. It was the signature event for initiating the transformation of Healing U, and I wanted us to get it right. We followed the transformation process as Paul and I had discussed it, and as he suggested, I relied on our consultants to guide our process.

Our objectives for the Transformation Summit were to:

- Achieve a shared vision of what a transformed Healing U would look like
- Gain consensus on the guiding principles that will guide the transformation
- Develop and document an enterprise map to understand the highest level processes
- Identify and prioritize these high-level processes for transformation
- Review, validate, and/or complete the transformation governance process to include all leadership roles and responsibilities
- Identify and/or confirm the leadership and membership of all process transformation teams; officially charter them
- Develop a transformation master schedule

It was a very intense three days. We did it off site so that we would be able to fully immerse ourselves and provide our undivided attention to this critical event. I began the meeting, taking the opportunity to sincerely encourage our leadership team in this Lean transformation effort. I first described a not-so-pretty picture of our current performance, which of course everyone was already aware. Then I tried to connect us all to the Mission of Healing University—caring for the people in this underserved region. I shared with them the successes we had achieved with the revenue cycle and the emergency department Lean projects, and stated my view that this was The Way to ensure the health and future of our service to the community. Finally, I challenged them to join with me as we continued our pursuit of cultural transformation and operational excellence in support of Perfect Care.

I must have done a pretty good job with it. Afterward, a number of my leaders pulled me off to the side and told me that my impassioned call to action convinced them to join with me at both an intellectual and emotional level. They said I had won both their minds and their hearts. I don't consider myself a great speaker, so I was both surprised and humbled by their response. More importantly, I had achieved their commitment.

During the next portion of the Transformation Summit, we developed a shared Vision of what we wanted Healing U to be. We engaged in some team exercises that helped us crystallize our vision from a variety of shareholder perspectives. We developed a vision for what we wanted Healing U to be to our team members, our physicians, the community, and most importantly, our patients. This turned out to be an exciting and energizing exercise, and one which would guide us into the future. The Vision we came up with for our Patients was particularly enlightening. (*see next page*)

As each team completed its work, key elements and consistent themes were identified. These were integrated into a model depicting a Vision of a Transformed Healing University Healthcare system. (*see next page*)

Vision for Our Patients

- ❑ Organized – They were expecting me
- ❑ Consistent service standard
- ❑ Patient-centered care team works together/seamless care
- ❑ Easy access
- ❑ They know me here
- ❑ My needs will be met
- ❑ They care about my family
- ❑ They listen to me
- ❑ I feel safe
- ❑ They have technically competent and compassionate team
- ❑ I trust Healing University Hospital
- ❑ Right thing at the right time
- ❑ Accurate, compassionate
- ❑ The best care
- ❑ Anticipating my needs
- ❑ It's all about me
- ❑ We have been waiting for you!

Our Vision of a Transformed Healing U

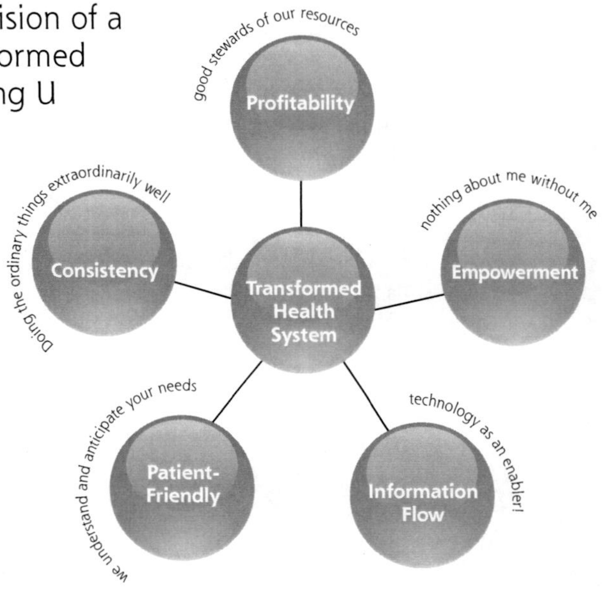

We concluded the first day by developing a set of Guiding Principles for the Transformation. These established our high-level objectives and the activities and behaviors that we would adhere to.

Staying true to the insights I had achieved in my discussions with Paul, we concluded that the ultimate objective of our Transformation was to Standardize Best Practices. The team was also enthused by the phrase "The Healing Way" to describe the standardized way that we perform Best Practices, so we incorporated both these concepts into our Guiding Principles:

People Transformation: Participative Culture and Engaged Partners

- Best Leadership Practices developed and implemented across the system
- Culture of performing in accordance with "The Healing Way"
- Culture of continual improvement
- Engaged and empowered team members
- Aligned physician partners

Process Transformation: Operational Excellence

- The Healing Way: Best Clinical and Business Practices identified
- "The Healing Way" documented in policies and procedures
- "The Healing Way" implemented consistently across the system
- Consistent adherence to "The Healing Way" by all staff and physicians

After that we called it a day. We were quite satisfied with our accomplishments, and excited to put a plan together to achieve the Vision we had developed.

I had a board meeting that evening. Among other agenda items, I planned to present fourth quarter and annual results. At this point I had been around for nearly a year, and we were starting to make measurable progress. I was looking forward to sharing our progress with the board, and especially our Chairwoman, Eileen Markum.

Eileen was a prominent local businesswoman. She was a brilliant entrepreneur, and one of the first to see the promise of the burgeoning internet economy. She seized the opportunity and grew her regional retail group into a national player. In addition to being a visionary entrepreneur, having grown up here she was also very involved in the community, and very passionate about Healing U and the care we provided to the community. She had watched its downfall with dismay, and joined the board to try to make a difference. Eileen was one of the major reasons I had taken the job. During my interview process I was impressed by both her intellect and her commitment to Healing U. I believed she would be a strong ally and supporter in our efforts to turn around the system. I was not mistaken.

Eileen opened the meeting, and invited me to present our financial report. We still lost money for the year, but operating results improved by over $6M. I was hoping to do a little better, but after the results of the prior three years it was clear that we were moving decisively in the right direction.

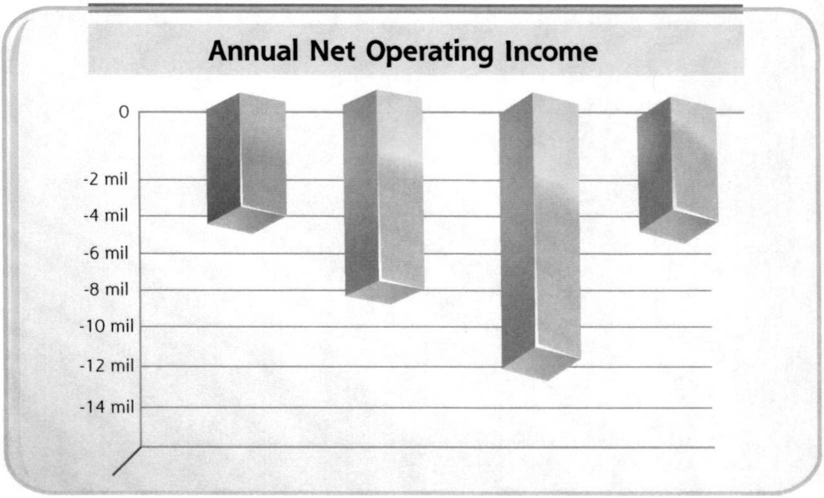

"Congratulations Will," Eileen said. "You seem to be moving things in the right direction. To what do you attribute this improvement?"

At a prior board meeting I had shared with them some preliminary results from the revenue cycle project, and took this opportunity to provide an update.

"Lana Davis and her team have done a great job," I began. "We continue to see improvements in overall collections. We're doing a lot better job of getting the appropriate patient information up front, including orders and accurate insurance information, and we initiated point-of-service cash collections. We have also significantly reduced the bottlenecks in our patient billing process, which significantly decreased our A/R days. The onetime cash acceleration due to shortening the A/R days was a significant factor in improving this year's results. I expect to see further improvement this year as revenue-cycle results flow through to the bottom line."

"Well done. Would you also please brief us on the Emergency Department Project?" Eileen asked, a grin broadening on her face. Eileen and the rest of the board members had no doubt seen our article in the paper. A couple of them took the opportunity to kid me a little bit about my "cowboy-fireman" picture. It wasn't as conservative an image as they might have liked for their hospital CEO, but they loved the message: "Empowered team members transform Healing U. ER—Patients praise improvements."

Eileen was already fully briefed on the project and this was an invitation for me to share additional information about the team's good work with the board.

"Gladly," I said, and showed them the chart depicting our reduction in Length of Stay.

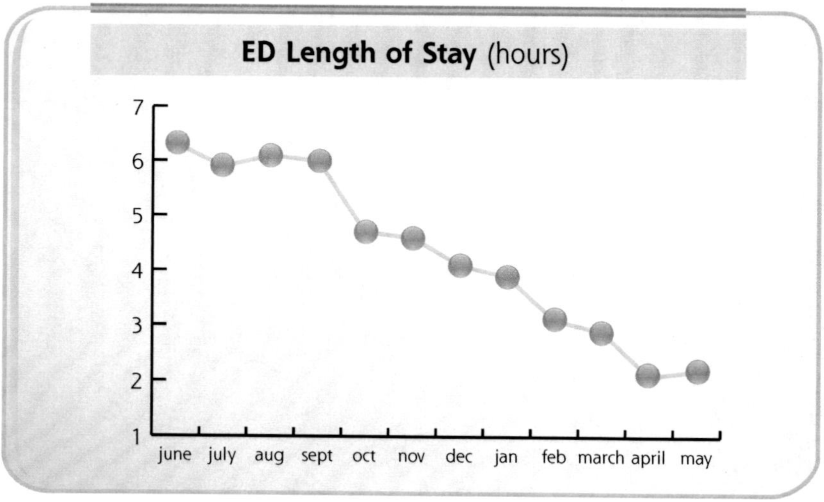

"We started using physicians in triage, which has significantly reduced our Left Without Being Seen. We also have had quite a bit of success getting our inpatients from the ED to the nursing units much more quickly. So we aren't losing patients who get tired of waiting, and consequently our inpatient volumes are higher. This has resulted in significant improvement to our bottom line," I said.

"You've been using Lean to improve your processes, right?" asked John Davis. John was an executive with a local automotive supplier, and was very familiar with the application of Lean to drive process improvement.

"We have," I confirmed.

"I wasn't sure that would work in healthcare," he observed. "People aren't widgets."

"Thank you for that observation, John," I said enthusiastically. It was a perfect opening for me to tell them all about our concept of Healing Pathways and the adaptations we had made to the traditional concepts of Value Streams and Value Stream Analysis. "Truth be told," I started, "health care processes are a lot more similar to production processes than we sometimes want to acknowledge. The same principles for improving the flow of processes apply, whether what is flowing is widgets, information, or people. But the difference with people is that they are not inanimate objects. Therefore, we must also consider their experience of the process, from their perspective. That is why we developed the concept of Healing Pathway Analysis. It is a Value Stream Analysis, plus. The 'plus' is that we look at the process from the patient's perspective."

"That's quite innovative" observed Eileen. Coming from the entrepreneurial innovator that she was, that was quite a humbling compliment for me.

"Thank you very much," I said. "I think the Healing Pathway concept has really helped us do a much better job of patient care, and our patient satisfaction results clearly demonstrated that." I showed them the latest patient satisfaction data for the Emergency Department. We were in the 99th percentile, and that was an accomplishment of which I was extremely proud.

John chimed in: "Well, it sounds like you should be doing more of it!"

"Thank you again John," I said with a broad smile. "You're setting me up perfectly tonight!" I took the opportunity to tell them about our Transformation Summit, and that by week's end we would have a plan for carrying out the Transformation across the system. I think the board was quite pleased. They dismissed me and went into Executive Session.

I waited in my office, and when the board meeting concluded Eileen and I met to debrief. She again congratulated me for the progress we were making, and let me know that the board had voted to extend my contract. "We're convinced you are on the right track, and are confident you will be able to return to profitability this year."

I was optimistic as well, and had said as much during the board meeting.

"But let me ask you a question, off the record," she said. "How do you really feel about our current level of patient care? Would you send your family members here?"

Eileen and I had this discussion before. Making Healing U a place we could recommend to our family and friends was the real measure of success for both of us.

"Off the record," I said wryly, "We can now do a great job registering and billing people!"

We both laughed. "That's helpful," she said.

"But seriously, I am very confident about our emergency care. I would rate us as high as anyone. Our staff and physicians are flourishing in the environment they have helped create, and are performing at extraordinarily high levels. As for the rest of our services, I know we can provide solid, quality care. But it's not near the level you and I both want it to be at. But I'm confident that it soon will be."

"I have every confidence in you, Will," Eileen said.

"Thanks," I said. "I'll keep you up to date." We said goodnight and went home to our families.

The Transformation Summit continued early the next morning. I briefed the team on the highlights of the board meeting, and expressed the board's appreciation for all their efforts. The board's relationship with the senior leadership team had been a bit strained over the past few years, so the change in tenor was a welcome development.

Next on the agenda was developing the Enterprise Map. An Enterprise Map is a high-level diagram of the internal services and activities of an organization. It shows the interdependencies between an organization's various patient care and support services, a necessary first step to keep us from sub-optimizing our improvement efforts.

The Black Belts engaged us in brainstorming and identifying all the key processes we performed. We generated the following list:

Healing U's Key Processes

- Revenue Cycle Front End: Central Scheduling/Registration/ Transcription
- Revenue Cycle Back End: Patient Accounting/HIM/ Reimbursement
- Case Management
- Surgical Services
- Nursing Electronic Medication Administration Record (EMAR)
- Emergency Department
- Supply Chain
- Med Imaging
- Electronic Medical Record (EMR) Clinical Data Repository
- Physician Systems (CPOE, EBM)
- Bed Control
- Financial Decision Support

- Physician Recruitment/Relations
- Pharmacy
- Laboratory
- Patient Safety
- Ambulatory Physician Practice Management
- Budget & Forecasting/Corporate Accounting
- HR (Workforce, Benefits, Education)
- Quality/Accreditation
- IT (Help Desk, Project Management)
- Infection Control
- Psych./Behavioral Health
- Dietary/Nutrition
- Contract Management
- Home Health
- Environmental Services
- Engineering
- Security Systems
- Pt. Transport
- Rehab
- Facility/Property Management
- Risk Management

Next we prioritized the processes to be transformed. We were asked to consider a number of factors, including:

- The impact on patient care
- The impact on throughput
- The impact on profitability
- Ease of transformation
- Availability of strong leader

Then we used a group voting process to come up with a prioritized ranking of processes to transform.

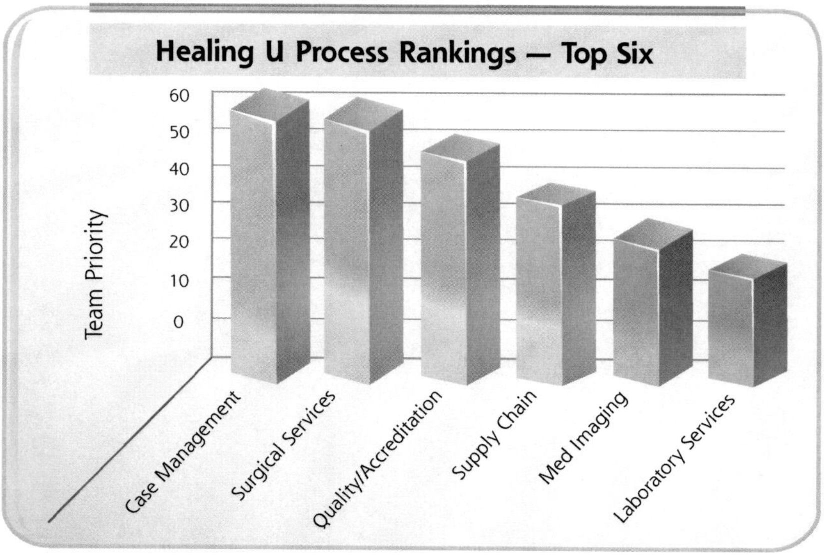

We prioritized a total of twenty-eight processes that we wanted to transform. Then, as we did with the revenue cycle and emergency department projects, we drafted a charter for each of the projects. Each charter identified:

- The name of the Healing Pathway/Value Stream to be transformed
- The purpose and key objectives of the project
- The business case
- The process boundaries: where the process began and ended
- Any constraints the team needed to be aware of, i.e., funding, FTEs, capital
- Team membership, including the executive sponsor, team leader, and team members.

Finally, we developed a schedule that sequenced the processes we would transform over the next twenty-four months. We hoped we might be able to do it more quickly, but we developed the schedule in a way that erred on the side of being conservative. We decided that we would do a total of six projects at a time, which was a somewhat arbitrary number but we wanted each of the six members of the Senior Leadership Team, myself included, to be involved as an Executive Sponsor of one project at a time. Perhaps more importantly, many of the projects would require the same participants so we couldn't overlap those projects. Developing a workable schedule was a bit of a challenge, but it paid off handsomely. It would also be useful in helping us ensure steady progress going forward.

At the end of the Summit, we were quite worn out. It was a very intense three days. We also shared the sense of accomplishment that comes with a job well done. That more than made up for any temporary exhaustion. We had developed a plan that we were all comfortable with and that we were mutually committed to. We believed that we had laid the foundation for our turn-around and we were excited to go forth and make it happen.

When I got home that night Tyler was already in bed but Amy was still up and working on some kind of list.

"Hi, honey," she chirped. "How'd the big meeting go today?"

"It was pretty draining but it went really well! We've got big plans for Healing U. It's going to take a while but we've got a good grasp on what our teams need to be doing. We are all pretty darn excited! What are you up so late working on?" I asked.

"Well, you know Tyler's fifth birthday is next month and you promised me we could have a nice backyard barbecue with one of those blowup bouncy things that kids love so much. I'm just working on a guest list for it."

"Oh, great! I was thinking, maybe we could get a clown to come too, or are kids scared of those these days?" I remembered I used to love clowns when I was a kid, but ever since Stephen King's "IT" came out, people seemed to have an aversion to clowns.

"Well, we can talk about that later. What I wanted to ask you is if you would feel comfortable having your mom and Paula come in town for the party? Your mom's been dropping not-so-subtle hints that she'd like to come in town for a long weekend. It's been so long since we've seen her. I thought this would be a great time for her to come."

I was initially taken aback by this suggestion. I knew the day would come when mom would want to come down for a visit, but her heart attack last year really gave me a scare. I had put off asking her to visit because I was afraid something might happen to her while she was here visiting. I didn't trust Healing U to be able to take care of someone so near and dear to me. Amy and I had discussed this on a couple different occasions.

"Well," I offered, "We have made great strides in the ED, haven't we? The time between being seen in the ER and getting to that cath lab is under thirty minutes for heart patients. I know I would trust us to take care of mom if, heaven forbid, she were to have another heart attack. And our patient satisfaction is at the 99th percentile. I think her experience would rival what she had at Mercy! Yes, you're right, Amy. I think I am comfortable with it. In fact, it sounds like a great idea. I'll call tomorrow and ask her and Paula to come down."

Mom and Paula did end up coming down for Tyler's big day. Everyone had a really great time, scary clown and all. As importantly, I was beginning to become comfortable with the care we were providing at Healing U. I was glad we didn't need to utilize their services during mom's trip but was happy to realize that things were now going well enough that I would trust us with family and friends, in case of an emergency.

Chapter EIGHTEEN

Follow Up and Follow Through

Paul called a few days later. I noted with interest the evolution in our relationship. Initially I was clearly the junior member of the pair—the student—and he the wise teacher. But over time the relationship had changed. First of all, we had gotten to be pretty good friends. We had developed a mutual respect for each other, and enjoyed our conversations on a personal level. In addition, my growing knowledge and experience with organizational transformation had allowed us to become more like peers. We now sometimes got into more advanced discussions where there wasn't necessarily a right answer, or if there was, neither of us knew it.

Today was one of those days. We were engaged in discussing the finer points of maintaining the energy and excitement of transformation events, specifically Healing Pathway analyses and Transformation Summits. During our conversations, Paul had clearly made the point, which I accepted, that follow up was most critical to success—and where many organizations fail in their transformation efforts. I had seen that for myself with our initial revenue-cycle project. Since then, I was very intentional about follow-up and follow-through to ensure implementation of the plans that were developed during the Value Stream and Healing Pathway analyses.

Now the challenge was even greater: ensuring follow-up and follow-through on the comprehensive plan we developed at the Transformation Summit. I had already given it a lot of thought, so I had a pretty good understanding of what I wanted to do. I welcomed the opportunity to use Paul as my sounding board.

"Here's what I'm thinking," I began. "We've got a plan. We have identified the projects, sponsors and team members. We have a schedule. Now we need to make sure the plan gets executed. So it seems to me we will need some metrics that indicate our progress, and a regular review of those metrics."

"Go on," encouraged Paul.

"It also seems to me that these will just be measures of activity. In other words, are we engaged in the transformation efforts that we planned at the Summit? But they don't tell us anything about how well we are achieving actual results.

"I agree," said Paul. "I have seen some organizations rely too heavily on measures of activity—how many events they are having, how many people are involved, etc.—and not enough on outcomes."

"Exactly," I continued. "Outcomes is a good word for it. We need to measure both: (a) deployment—the depth and breadth of the enterprise transformation across the organization; and (b) outcome—the organizational impacts achieved through the deployment effort.

"And your senior leadership team needs to review both on a regular basis," said Paul, completing my thought.

"You got it," I agreed. "Getting together on a regular basis to review deployment and outcome results will enable us to monitor the transformation, identify and remove barriers, and keep the team energized and on track."

Talking further, Paul and I concluded that there were two distinct but interdependent levels at which we would collect and review data: the Enterprise level, and the Healing Pathway/Value Stream level. We further concluded that it would make sense to look at outcome and deployment measures at each of these levels.

At the enterprise level, we already had many key outcome measures that were reviewed on a regular basis. These were the operating metrics most hospitals would monitor, including clinical quality, labor costs, supply costs, A/R days, financials, etc. But we didn't currently have them organized into a single dashboard that we could use for regular, at-a-glance monitoring of the overall health of our organization. I decided to do that, and came up with the following:

Healing University Medical Center
Enterprise Dashboard

OUTCOME MEASURES	Favorable Values	July	Aug	Sept	Oct	Nov	Dec	YTD Act.
CLINICAL QUALITY								
Unadjusted overall mortality rate	Lower	3.14%	2.27%	2.20%	2.35%	2.30%	2.45%	2.45%
Significant adverse events	Lower	1	0	0	1	0	1	7
%Readmissions 30 days/Medicare	Lower	15.91%	15.33%	14.60%	14.34%	14.10%	14.15%	14.74%
Hospital acquired conditions (occurrences)	Lower	2	4	6	4	4	3	23
CLINICAL UTILIZATION								
Adjusted discharges	Higher	3132	2858	3210	3033	3045	2876	40,337
Medicare case mix index	Higher	1,318	1,418	1,378	1,407	1,473	1,433	1,836
Total ALOS (CMI Adjusted)	Lower	2468	2300	2221	2060	2216	2241	2251
REVENUE CYCLE								
Gross AR days	Lower	59.9	59.5	58.6	54.3	56.0	56.4	57.435
Cash as a % of net patient revenue	Higher	2.75	2.89	2.45	2.98	2.81	2.90	2.798
LABOR								
Paid FTEs	Lower	3,108	2,946	2,967	2,928	2,892	2,747	2,931
Work FTEs	Lower	2,637	2,697	2,698	2,548	2,485	2,310	2562
Paid FTEs per adj. discharge	Lower	0.45	0.46	0.42	0.43	0.43	0.43	0.436
Salary & Wages as % of Net Patient Rev	Lower	38.7%	39.4%	40.1%	38.4%	39.1%	39.4%	39.2%
Overtime as % of Salaries	Lower	0.8%	0.7%	0.8%	0.8%	0.8%	0.08%	0.8%
NON-LABOR								
Sup. & pur. service $ per adj. discharge	Lower	1550.38	171762.93	1734.16	1604.93	1623.41	1892.28	1694.68
Sup. & pur. service $ per adj. patient day	Lower	297.33	344.93	342.53	331.85	315.14	375.02	334.47
Drug costs per adj. patient day	Lower	54.81	66.60	61.01	56.82	45.21	58.22	57.11
Supply costs as % of Net Patient Revenue	Lower	8.6%	9.9%	9.4%	9.8%	8.6%	9.9%	9.4%
HUMAN RESOURCES								
Benefits expenses per adj. discharge	Lower	1125.62	1066.31	1264.52	1011.95	1020.77	1008.53	1082.95
Salary & wages per adj. discharge	Lower	4452.16	4414.20	4713.75	4285.62	4420.64	4310.42	4432.80
Premium pay exp. per adj. discharge	Lower	195.46	180.54	171.43	165.19	164.00	211.93	181.42
FINANCIAL STRENGTH								
Net patient revenue per adj. discharge	Higher	13516.24	13529.68	14484.22	12618.20	13612.38	14317.03	13679.63
Total costs per adjusted discharge	Lower	12269.73	12780.95	13072.17	11773.31	12201.31	12391.41	12414.76
Operating Margin %	Higher	3.0%	3.5%	5.0%	4.4%	3.7%	4.0%	3.9%

With regard to deployment at the Enterprise level, the Transformation Master Schedule that we had developed during the Summit would serve our needs perfectly.

At the Healing Pathway/Value Stream level, the charters for each project provided a starting point for the outcome measures we should track. These were identified in the "Purpose and Key Objectives" portion of the charter. Desired outcome metrics for each project would be further refined during the respective Healing Pathway/Value Stream analyses. The Executive Sponsor for each would be charged to develop a dashboard of all outcome metrics for that Pathway.

Healing University Medical Center
Surgical Services Healing Pathway

METRICS	Baseline	GOAL	May	June	July	August	Sept	Oct
QR Turn Over Time	35 min	25 min	36	34	32	24	23	22
1st Case Ontime	73%	80%	65%	64%	53%	77%	74%	78%
Worked Hrs/100 min	14.2%	12.28	13.4	13.4	13.6	12.24	12.0	11.93
Suite Utilization 7a - 11p	60%	75%	61%	61%	57%	104%	88%	84%

With regard to monitoring deployment at this level, the Rapid Improvement Plan developed during the initial Healing Pathway/Value Stream analysis would serve that purpose well.

"That sounds great," said Paul. "Do you anticipate a relationship between the outcome measures at the enterprise level and at the Healing Pathway/Value Stream level?"

We both knew it was a rhetorical question, but worth discussing nonetheless. "Of course," I said. "Ultimately, what we are trying to move are the enterprise level metrics. They represent our performance against our organizational priorities, and are the ultimate measures of the success—or failure—of our efforts. Each Healing Pathway or Value Stream project should improve processes that are in alignment with our organizational priorities. That means they should have direct impact on our enterprise level metrics. If they don't, we are working on the wrong things."

"Well said," Paul responded. "And I'm sure you know why I asked?"

I suspected I did, and shared my thoughts with him.

"Exactly," he concurred. "In so many organizations that pursue improvement efforts, it seems to be something they simply add on to what they are already doing. They don't strategically determine the projects they should engage in. Consequently, they often choose projects that are not of most significance to the organization and thus fail to positively impact any enterprise level measures. It's much like the approach I learned NOT to use when I first tried implementing TQM: we trained people and then told them to go out and start improving projects. They did, but didn't always choose those projects that would impact the most important organizational objectives. We sub-optimized."

"And then, not seeing the benefits, they throw the baby out with the bath water," I added. "I get it. We will be best served by applying our improvement efforts strategically, using them as a tool to improve the processes and measures most important to us. That is why our Healing Pathway and Value Stream metrics should be in alignment with our organizational metrics."

I continued: "We'll review these metrics during follow-up meetings that we've scheduled on a bi-weekly basis over the next few months." Paul had driven this point home in our prior conversations, and I had come to believe that this follow up was critical to ensuring the sustainability of the enterprise transformation effort. "The team decided to call these our 'Transformation Support' meetings," I said. "I kind of like it."

"I think you have arrived, my son," said Paul kiddingly, but in a way that acknowledged that we had, indeed, begun to become peers who could learn from each other.

"I'm getting there," I said honestly. It was a good conversation.

Our first Transformation Support meeting was held two weeks later. As planned, it was a four-hour session that included each member of the Senior Leadership Team. As the Executive Sponsors of their respective projects, their participation was mandatory. Team leaders were also welcome to participate. We resolved to make these interactive, problem-solving sessions, rather than mere 'data dumps.' We had the right leaders in the room to understand the complexities of any obstacles and to determine a way forward as needed. Enabling the transformation was why we were taking this time to meet, and we wanted to use it effectively.

We followed an agenda that became our gold standard for Transformation Support meetings:

- CEO welcome and remarks
- Review status of prior action items
- Review enterprise operational dashboard
- Identify any opportunity areas; assign responsibility
- Review enterprise deployment progress
- Review each active Healing Pathway/Value Stream initiative
- Solve problems and eliminate barriers
- Evaluate and re-prioritize initiatives as appropriate
- Review and summarize new action items

At this first Transformation Support meeting there was a lot of good news to report. Of the six projects we were currently leading, five had already had their Healing Pathway or Value Stream Analysis. The other was scheduled for early the next week. Huge opportunities had been identified. Rapid Improvement Plans were developed, along with schedules for conducting the follow-on Rapid Improvement Events, Projects, and Just-Do-Its. There was a lot of excitement and energy in the room.

Lana, our CFO, was an old hand at this by now. She acted as the team leader on our very first event, the revenue cycle, on which I served as Executive Sponsor. So she already had a little experience and a big success under her belt. Right now she was leading the Supply Chain project. Financially, it was one of our most critical, and I was confident in her ability to get excellent results there.

After Don Baird left the organization, we promoted Cheryl Gateway to Chief Nursing Officer. She had been with Healing U for over 20 years, and worked her way up from floor nurse. She was passionate about patient care, and volunteered to lead the case management effort project. It was focused on better coordinating patient care to improve their inpatient experience and get them home sooner. What she lacked in Lean experience she made up for in interpersonal skills and credibility with the docs and staff. I was sure that, with the right coaching and mentoring, she would do just fine.

Tim, our COO, had a successful project under his belt. When Baird left, Tim took over responsibility for the Emergency Department project. I was a little concerned, since he seemed to be a bit of a skeptic, but he later told me the success of the rev cycle project had convinced him the value of the Lean approach. Ultimately, the ED project was a great success. Tim was now tackling the surgical services area. We had plenty of opportunities there. As I had heard from our physicians on numerous occasions, our surgeries didn't start on time, we weren't organized, and staffing was a challenge. From an operational perspective, productivity was horrible which meant labor costs were horrible as well. Lots of opportunities, and I knew Tim would relish the challenge and get great results.

Dr. Margie Salmon, our CMO, had the quality & accreditation project. This was a huge opportunity for us. Maggie's project included improving the delivery of excellent patient care, and based on what I had learned over the last year and a half that required a stable quality management system, so we also included that as part of the project. Maggie had her work cut out for her. My biggest concern with Maggie was her lack of leadership experience. But she was hardworking, smart, and a great competitor. I knew she would do everything in her power to be successful, and in my view, all that was going to take was a little coaching on my part.

Denise, our Chief Administrative Officer, had the lead on the medical imaging project. At one time she was the director of that department, so she had significant technical experience there. In terms of doing her duty, Denise was the best 'soldier' I had. I knew she would do her darnedest to do what the boss wanted. I was hopeful that she, too, would be successful.

I had the Lab project. Historically it had been a bottleneck for many of our patient services, and I was committed to making it flow much more smoothly. We had a new lab director, Aaron Els, and he had already brought a lot of innovation and change to the lab. He would be the Team Leader for the project. I felt pretty good about our chances of success there.

We all made our reports. It was too early in the process to report either success or failure, except to indicate whether or not we were accomplishing the HPAs and VSAs as planned. We looked forward to our next meeting in two weeks. We were hopeful we might have more substance to report by then.

We met again as scheduled, and followed our same agenda. First on the agenda was follow-up on the action items we had assigned at our prior meeting. Items captured here were not those that were already in our transformation plan, or the rapid improvement plans for the Healing Pathways and Value Streams. Rather, these were actions required to address barriers or accomplish other tasks that we may not have anticipated.

One such action item from the prior meeting was Dr. Salmon's. Cheryl needed her help on the case management project. Dr. Salmon was supposed to follow up with the internists, doc to doc, to get them to follow the new process for referrals to specialists. She had met with them, but they were still not following the new process. We explored the issue together, as a leadership team, to determine how to best resolve the issue. Dr. Salmon indicated that she had explained the new process to them, and asked them to comply with it. The internists told her in no uncertain terms that they were not going to "sacrifice their clinical judgment just to save a few bucks." However, the data showed that they called in 60 percent more specialists per patient than the industry norms, and we had strong suspicions that they were calling in physician friends of theirs for consults whether they were clinically indicated or not.

Dr. Salmon indicated that she was very willing to draw a line in the sand and require their compliance. She firmly believed it was the right thing to do, and didn't like the fact that we had no organizational control over the practice habits of docs in our system. But she also indicated she was a little hesitant to do so as she thought they might leave the organization. Through further discussion I learned that Healing U had a history of giving the docs whatever they wanted when such threats occurred. I also learned that under the prior administration Dr. Salmon had once tried to be firm, only to have her decision overturned when the docs went over her head. In that light, she was rightfully concerned about whether we would have her back; and whether we were willing to risk losing docs.

Cheryl and Tim both reiterated that compliance was not an option, and that they would support Dr. Salmon. I concurred. We encouraged her to revisit the internists and give them a deadline for compliance, after which their privileges would be suspended. We assured her that this was a consensus executive team decision, and that we would have her back. Assured of our support, Dr. Salmon was very comfortable in having the follow-up meeting, and politely but firmly communicated the organization's expectations. To be on the safe side, we also assigned Cheryl the responsibility for coming up with a backup plan should the docs choose to leave.

As it turned out, both internists stayed, but not after trying to go around Dr. Salmon in every way possible. To our credit, the team stuck together and presented a unified and strong front—much like two parents that do not let their children divide and conquer them! It was the first time we had been tested as we strove for transformation, but it wouldn't be the last.

We later learned something that was obvious to us in hindsight: most of the docs in our organization were very willing to play by the rules. They were dedicated, hard-working people that entered the profession to care for patients. What they didn't like was the fact that some docs abused the system and that administration let them get away with it. It violated their sense of fairness—and rightfully so. If Dr. X wasn't going to play by the rules, then why should they?

Ultimately we lost a couple docs over the course of our transformation, but based on the reports from our patients, our team members, and especially our other physicians, we were far better off without them.

We reviewed our enterprise dashboard, but it was still too early to start seeing results there. The Healing Pathway and Value Stream projects were all making good progress, and we knew those results would soon start hitting the dashboard. We adjourned and looked forward to sharing our progress at our next meeting.

The next time the transformation support team met, we did start to see results at the project and organizational levels. Still relatively small, but they grew over time as we fully implemented our plan. We checked in on the teams' progress, identified and eliminated barriers, and kept ourselves and our organization on task.

At some point in the transformation, it seemed like we hit an emotional lull. It was quite an interesting phenomenon. The further we got into the transformation, the more we lost the initial excitement and energy that was engendered at the Transformation Summit. This phenomenon was mirrored at the Healing Pathway and Value Stream levels: the initial excitement of the three-day events eventually wore off.

In retrospect, that left us in a danger zone of sorts, wondering at times whether we were on the right course. I knew we were, but I too felt a little unsettled, a little doubtful, and wanted to hear it from Paul. He told me that this is the point at which many organizations abandon their transformation efforts. They have done the hard work of planning and setting up the transformation infrastructure, but they are not yet seeing the results. Commitment wanes. They don't realize how close they are to success; they don't maintain the drumbeat of follow up and follow through. The initiative fails. The team is demoralized. Nothing changes.

We stayed the course. Once we started seeing results, we experienced a perhaps more grounded and enduring energy and excitement—that of success. It was different. It seemed a more mature and worthy excitement, based on mutual accomplishment and not just the social energy generated during the three-day events. I marveled at the motivation our success engendered in me, my team, and our organization. Success does beget success.

Unfortunately, Denise Mariner, our Chief Administrative Officer, was not having the same success that the other leaders were. With responsibility for IT, Supply Chain, and Engineering, she had perhaps a little greater scope of responsibility for our Lean Transformation than her peers. Her functions were system-wide, and necessarily involved most of the transformation efforts in one way or another.

Having said that, we had assembled a tremendous amount of resources under her, including the subject matter experts and Black Belts just as we had provided for every team. But in addition to that, since she was over IT and the installation of the new HIS, she also had the benefit of a significant amount of help and expertise from the new IT vendor and independent IT consultants, all of whom were very competent and experienced in system-wide implementations. So I didn't think workload was the issue. She had demonstrated a great capacity for managing multiple projects and responsibilities in the past.

But she seemed to be struggling, with regard to transformation results, and also emotionally. She just didn't seem to be as energized as the rest of us were. Instead, she seemed stressed and irritable.

"How's it going, Denise?" I asked during our private weekly meeting.

"Just Great!" she said, mustering as much enthusiasm as she could.

"You seem to be struggling a bit," I suggested empathetically, trying to give her an opening.

"Oh, I just have some personal stuff going on," she offered. "No big deal."

"Oh, ok," I said. The way she said it convinced me that she didn't care to talk about it, so I didn't push her on how she was doing personally. I wanted to honor her boundaries. So I shifted to work performance.

"Your transformation efforts don't seem to be progressing well," I observed.

"Don't worry boss," she said with genuine respect. "We are working through some challenges but we will get there."

That was certainly Denise's style. She was hard-working, respectful, and chain-of-command; and she was still the one I went to if I really needed something done. I resolved to let it go for now and follow up in a couple weeks.

In the meantime, I began to get some feedback from our IT vendor and consultants on Denise's leadership style. It seems she was being more command-and-control than participative. Taking what they said with a grain of salt, I checked with some of our key team members. While reluctant to say anything negative about their boss, they did say enough for me to understand that she was not embracing the new culture of empowerment that we were trying to achieve. She was being very directive, even about things of which she did not have the necessary knowledge and expertise. This helped explain why the projects under her leadership were not progressing as well as they could have.

Upon reflection, I also began to understand the source of her angst and lack of professional enthusiasm and excitement about the transformation. She had professionally "grown up" at Healing U, and until recently the leadership environment was command and control. So naturally people that could function in that environment stayed, and like Denise, rose in the leadership ranks. This was an environment that seemed to value obedience over performance, and I could see that in Denise. The genuine respect she showed me is precisely what she wanted her subordinates to show her. She did not expect to be questioned, perhaps fearing that she would look weak if she didn't know everything; and she was cautious about forming any sort of personal relationship with her direct reports.

I could also see the state of cognitive dissonance I had created in her. She was conflicted by my expectation that she change her leadership style. On one hand, she was very respectful and clearly wanted to do what her boss wanted. On the other hand, it was contrary to her very fiber to empower her people and develop an atmosphere of mutual trust and respect. She had learned to manage by instilling fear in her people.

The question was which would win out: her duty to meet her boss's expectations, or her well-ingrained management style? I thought she was worth saving, and hoped it would be the former.

The next time we met, I shared my observations with her. She seemed a little uncomfortable at first, but we eventually did have what I thought was a very good discussion. She acknowledged the struggle she was having, but said "you're the boss," and assured me she was working on it. Together we identified some specific behavioral objectives for how she would modify her leadership style, and she reiterated her commitment to change. I wanted to give her every opportunity to be successful.

I believed, and still believe, that she was sincere in that commitment. She just couldn't do it. Two weeks later she tendered her resignation. She said she wanted to spend more time with her family, but I understood that there was more to it than that. In spite of her best efforts and intentions, she was just not able to change her leadership style. I wished her the best.

People deal with change in different ways. Some, like Don Baird, don't think they need to change. Rather, in their arrogance, they think the problem is everyone else. Others, like Denise, are willing, but find themselves unable to do so. I later found out that Denise had taken another CAO job out of state. It was a much more traditional organization, and was not in the process of change. I suspected that was a good fit for her, and I am sure she is doing a good job for them.

Over the next year and a half, the Transformation Support Team continued the drumbeat of bi-weekly meetings. The process continued much as it started: reviewing organizational and project status, identifying obstacles, moving the transformation forward. There were no sacred cows, no off-limit topics. We fearlessly identified issues, discussed them openly and honestly in an environment of mutual respect, and arrived at solutions. We maintained our focus; we made decisions; we eliminated barriers. We grew in mutual trust and respect as a leadership team. These were my people; and this was our process for ensuring the success of the transformation.

Chapter NINETEEN

Transformation Results - The New Healing U

To be honest, I was surprised at how smoothly it went once we got going. In retrospect, it seems that laying the groundwork by doing the Revenue Cycle and Emergency Departments projects first was exactly the right move. It enabled us to learn a few lessons, develop "pull" in the organization, and get the right people on the team. From there, the Transformation Summit propelled us forward.

It wasn't always smooth, and it wasn't always easy. There were fits and starts. Sometimes we moved quickly; at other times slowly; and sometimes we even went backwards. But we also persevered. We adhered to the first of Deming's 14 points:

- "Maintain a Constancy of Purpose"

Suffice it to say that over the next couple years we visited and transformed every one of our key support and delivery processes. I learned more than I ever thought there could be to learn. Not just about Lean and process improvement. But in truth, about how a hospital works, about the system in which our people work, and even about the human spirit, as I watched the subtle transformation of our team members. Through our transformation, our processes truly were transformed. But the transformation of our people was nothing short of amazing—from oftentimes being frustrated cogs in a wheel of complexity and dysfunction to energized, motivated, contributing entrepreneurs. People came to own their processes and tirelessly strove for continual improvement of care in support of our collective mission of service to our patients.

Over the course of our transformation, there were an amazing number of discoveries. Many improvements were complex, requiring a significant amount of Rapid Improvement Events and Six Sigma Projects.

But many more were Just-Do-Its—"no brainers," once we got deep enough into the process to understand what was really going on.

Increased Imaging Capacity. Take the imaging team, for example. They were chartered with transforming our CT and MRI processes. Their Rapid Improvement Plan yielded seven RIEs, two projects, and five Just-Do-Its. But one of the Just-Do-Its alone got us an additional $340K of contribution margin. In the process of reviewing the schedule over the course of the VSA, the team identified an error in the amount of time slotted for an MRI. The error was corrected immediately, allowing for an additional five MRIs per day! Amazing! It also helped with our add-on scheduling challenges there.

Surgical Services Productivity. On the other end of the spectrum, there were productivity improvements in the surgical services areas. In this case, there was no single breakthrough that yielded great returns, but rather a steady accomplishment of opportunities identified during the Healing Pathway Analysis. The effort included designing staffing models to meet the direct labor benchmark of fifteen hours worked per unit of service. The information brought to light during the Lean events enabled the team to make incremental improvements over the course of a year, yielding an annualized financial impact of $627K.

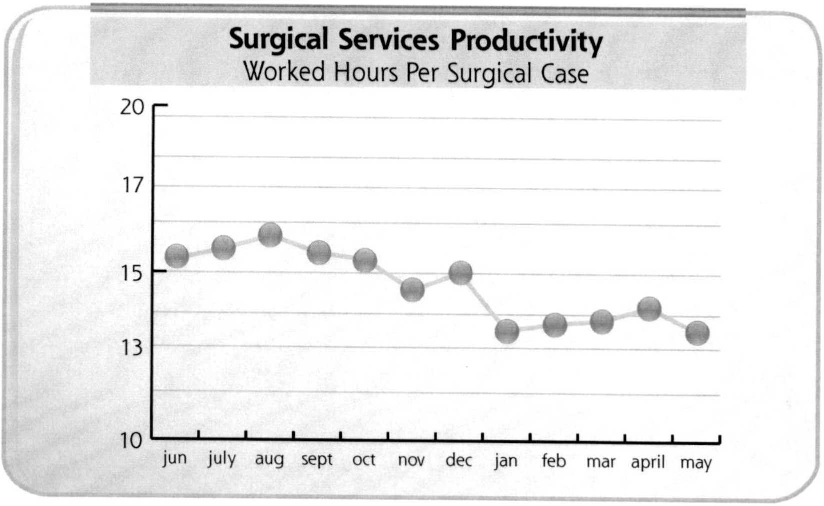

Reduced AMI Mortality. This project was particularly near and dear to me. The exceptional care my mother received at Mercy hospital was what first led me to Paul and this amazing journey. Given that experience, it was inevitable that one of our projects would focus on improving care of heart-attack patients. Our Cath Lab and ED Directors teamed up under the leadership of one of our Black Belts to improve the time to primary PCI for our patients. They conducted a Healing Pathway Analysis to identify opportunities, and implemented a number of improvements, including the following:

- The ED physician now interprets the EKG to determine patient disposition
- The ED physician contacts the cath lab personnel and the cardiologist
- The ED begins prepping the patient for the procedure
- The on-call cath lab nurse arrives at the ED and transports the patient to the cath lab
- The cath lab rooms were standardized to allow for faster stocking and set up of materials and supplies

By improving the coordination between the ED and the cath lab, the team reduced patient prep time and the time needed to get the patient into the cath lab for the procedure. Standardizing the cath lab rooms shortened the time required to get the procedure started. A Door to Balloon (D2B) team was created to facilitate the maintenance of the process, review each patient history for issues and implement additional process improvements as needed. As illustrated in the chart below, Healing U has significantly improved patient care, with 100 percent of our patients now receiving primary PCI with ninety minutes of arrival, and ZERO mortality rate. Awesome!

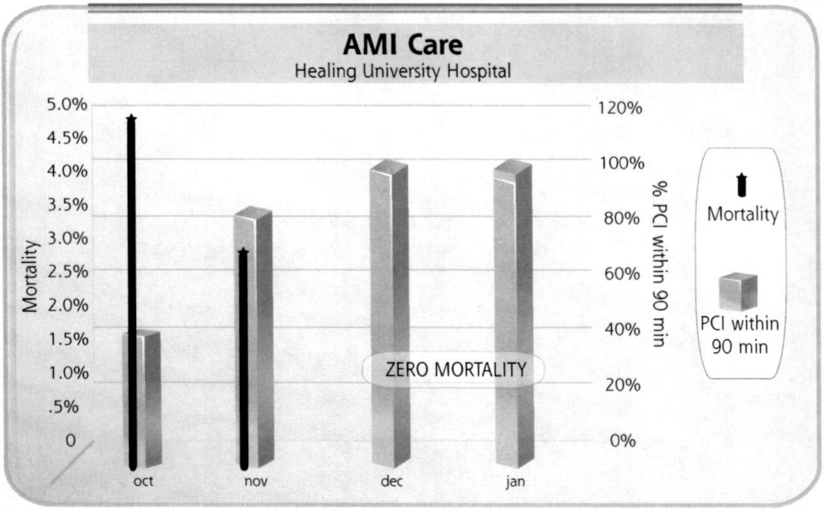

Medication Dispensing System. In another project we worked to improve appropriate utilization of our automated medication dispensing system. Stock-outs and discrepancies were major problems. Because of stock-outs, nurses and other staff hoarded supplies when they were available, so they would have them when they needed them. They were doing what they thought was in the best interests of their patients. Unfortunately, such hoarding created an appropriately called "hidden warehouse" of supplies on the units, and consequently created way too much inventory. The cause of the stock-outs was discrepancies. For example, the dispensing system might show that there were five widgets left in the machine, when there were actually only two. Consequently, when supply and distribution got the automated order to refill, the count was wrong and the supplies inadequate. The team determined that the root cause was that the staff were not coding every withdrawal from the system. So, for example, they might take medicines for multiple patients at once, but only code in one patient. And they only coded that one in because it was required to get the machine to open. Ergo, stock outs. Not to mention the lost patient billing since the items were not keyed to a specific patient!

We instituted a rigorous education program so the staff would understand the implications and consequences of not using the machines properly. Then we started publishing weekly scorecards, by cabinet, to monitor use. We saw a drastic change in inventory accuracy within the first month of scorecard use. Stock-outs were reduced 68 percent almost immediately. These improvements allowed us to realize an increase of $2,488,907 in gross charges, resulting in an impact of $273,780 to the bottom line. Increased billing doesn't do a lot for you with a prospective payment system, but there are still enough "percent of charge" payers to make it financially rewarding. And in critical access facilities that are cost-reimbursed, it makes all the difference in the world.

Orthopedic Implants. It can be quite challenging to do orthopedic im-

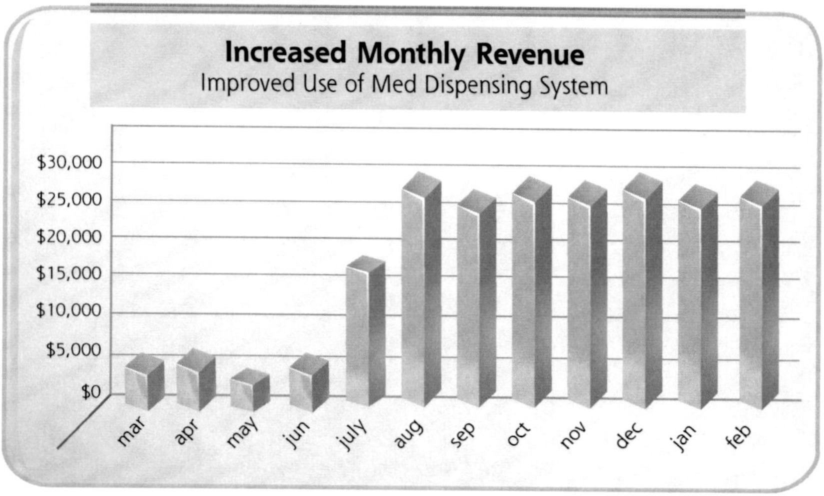

plants economically. Our efforts to reduce costs grew into a complex project with an interdisciplinary team including operations, supply, finance, physician hospital development, physicians, and performance improvement. It included data analyses to determine the strategic direction for negotiating price reductions on implants, negotiations with vendors, and numerous discussions with physicians. Eventually, the team's tremendous effort paid off. As depicted in the chart below, this project resulted in a total cost savings of a little over $1 million in the first year alone, with savings continuing into the future.

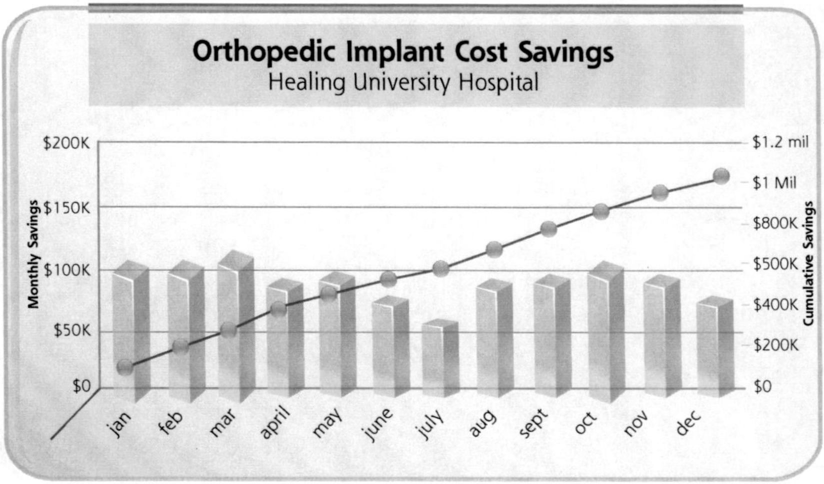

Prophylactic Antibiotic Administration. Under the leadership of the nurse manager of the surgical services group and the pharmacy director, a cross-functional team including physicians, surgical services, and the pharmacy set out to improve the administration of prophylactic antibiotics within one hour prior to surgical incision. Following the VSA, they conducted a series of RIEs during which they developed a standardized order set and a plan for minimizing the duplication of orders submitted to the pharmacy, designed a team member education plan for the processes, and created and implemented a rollout schedule for both the protocol documents and the processes necessary to use them. We continue to seek further improvement, but as shown in the graph below, we have made significant progress to date.

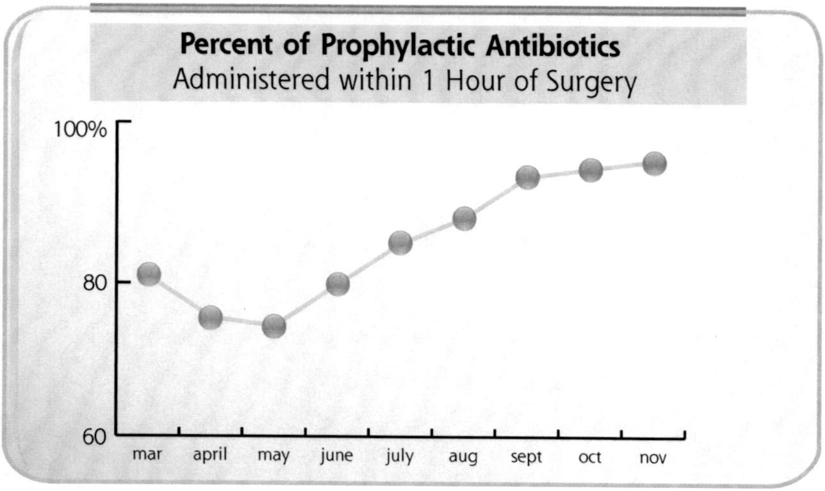

Overdue Invoices. Just prior to my arrival at Healing U we had outsourced supply management. After the transition we saw a significant spike in both RNI (Received Not Invoiced) and INR (Invoiced Not Received). As a result of the increase in past-due amounts, we were required to place $2 M in reserve to cover our outstanding debt. Of course, we were already strapped for cash, so this was a huge financial burden. The purchasing, materials management, and A/P teams joined in a concentrated effort to reduce past-due dollars and identify the root causes associated with the generation of excessive INR/RNI. Project efforts were focused on the matching process, where the invoice, PO and receiver are aligned to provide supplier payment. EDI interfaces were improved. The team's efforts resulted in a huge and sustained reduction in past-due amounts, resulting in a return of $1.8M of the reserve we had to place with the vendor, and also yielding a recurring benefit of $112K per annum.

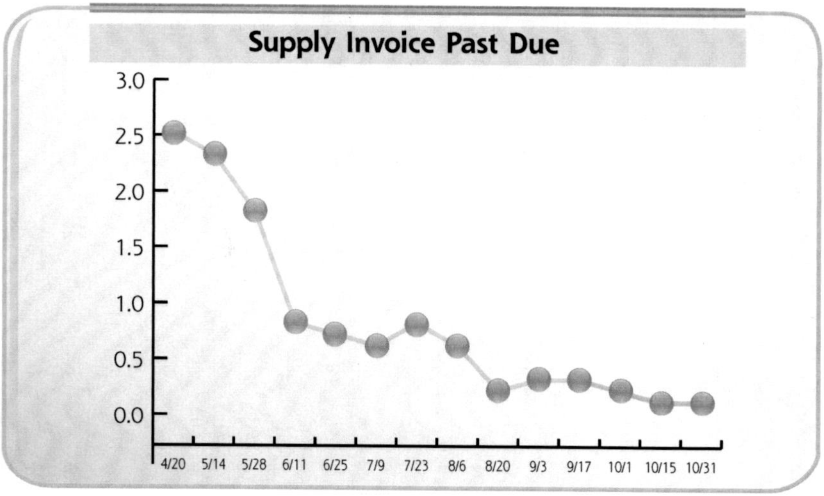

Inpatient Throughput. Another key initiative was inpatient throughput and reduced length of stay on the inpatient units. Minimizing the length of time a patient spends in the hospital is a practice that benefits both the patient and the hospital system. From the patient's perspective, one of the main reasons for reducing length of stay (LOS) is that it allows patients to be in the hospital only for the amount of time that is medically necessary. This helps them get home sooner and makes them less likely to acquire complications such as infections.

From the hospital's perspective, a shorter LOS assures the appropriate use of hospital resources. For instance, a reduction in LOS of just one-tenth of a day at Healing U is like opening up six new beds. Reducing LOS by a half-day is like opening a new thirty-bed unit. Adding new beds is costly ($1M each at a typical hospital). And CON (Certificate of Need) rules states that a hospital cannot add beds without state approval—at best a lengthy process. Reducing Length of Stay is therefore the best way to make more beds available. Ultimately, this allows more effective and efficient care to more patients.

For example, having more available in-patient beds means the Emergency Department doesn't have to go on diversion. It also ensures that beds will be available for post-op surgical needs, eliminating the backup in surgery. Direct admits and transfers don't back up in the admitting area. In addition, an appropriate LOS helps nursing and other services align their staffing to appropriate levels.

The team coined the name "bed flow" to describe what they were trying to achieve. The bed flow team included the CMO, care management, nursing, physicians, transportation, bed board, and environmental services. They implemented the following improvements:

- Eliminated the daily bed huddle and implemented an automated tracking system to update the status of each unit. This allows the RNs to remain on the unit.
- Developed a policy for closing, blocking, cleaning, and opening beds. The policy describes who can block a bed and when, eliminating the issue of opening a unit with dirty beds.
- Implemented discharge appointments for appropriate patient populations.
- Opened a clinical call center. The care manager in the bed control room appropriately places patients and level of care, ensures the transfers that we receive are placed in the appropriate unit, and that Healing University has an appropriate placement for the patient.
- Resumed using Code Gray for critical capacity management.

When the number of available beds gets too low at any level of care, a Code Gray announcement gathers the nurse managers to look for any discharges that can be appropriately expedited.

Over the last three years we have continued to improve our LOS. This has enabled us to provide a better patient experience and better patient care, and has also helped improve our bottom line. As Paul made me keenly aware by showing me the data, decreased length of stay is one of the most powerful enablers of improvement to the bottom line. In our organization, every 0.1 day reduction yields and additional $317k to the bottom line. That's huge for a system the size of Healing University.

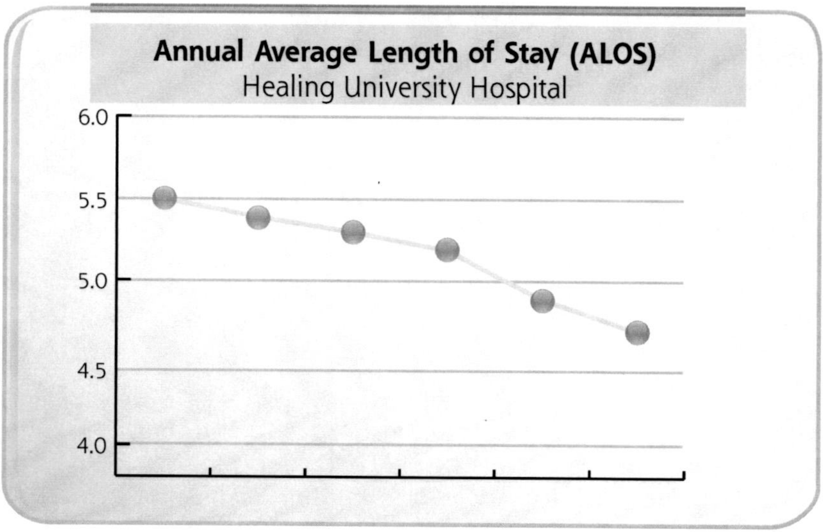

Numerous Intangible Benefits. Most of our improvement projects produced results that readily yielded a measurable improvement in patient care, physician or team member satisfaction, or impact to the bottom line. However, some projects yielded tremendous value with benefits that were not easily measured. Deming, the statistician-psychologist-philosopher, profoundly described the impact of these projects as "unknown and unknowable."

In the case of Healing U, even though we can't quantify the human impact in terms of dollars, what we do know is that these projects added significant value to our patients, our team members, and our processes. Following is a sampling of such projects we engaged in:

- **RAC Audits** — Conducted a Lean event to determine and document how Healing U will respond to the Recovery Audit Contractor process.
- **Advanced Research** — Conducted an event to review and redesign the process by which we accept and follow research studies.

- **Cath Lab** — Conducted an event to reallocate stocking and charge reconciliation procedures; and developed a data sheet to identify and track turn-around-time.
- **Environmental Services** — Developed a team member training video; instituted room cleaning audit and tracking sheet.
- **MRI** — Conducted a study to determine medical imaging capacity for each facility; analyzed CT and MRI contrast and lab draw costs for all facilities to assist with point of collection testing analysis.
- **Sterile Processing** — Conducted an analysis of sterilization and material flows yielding significant improvement in capacity.
- **PAT** — Created a process flow for first case and pre-access testing processes.
- **Surgical Services** — Conducted numerous 5S projects in the ORs and Sub-Sterile areas resulting in quicker room turnover and reduced supply costs.
- **Web page for Supply Chain Management (SCM)** — Designed and built a web page for the Healing University system to interface with SCM. The web page includes features such as: a contact list, methods to offer feedback/ask questions, methods to request reports, item conversion status, a policy/procedure bank, and a calendar for key SCM events (warehouse closures, early delivery times, etc.).
- **Going Green** — Initiated a Going Green effort. Key elements include toner, cell phone, plastic, aluminum, cardboard, and battery recycling.
- **Education/Training Standardization** — Worked to standardize and re-design our education/training program. This involved "Best Practice" research, as well as a two day Lean event with thirty-five team members associated with education departments throughout the system to develop the future state of the Healing U education system.
- **Position Description Standardization** — Conducted a Rapid Improvement Event to standardize our seven hundred eighty three active job titles, of which only one hundred eighty five were occupied by two or more team members.

I could go on and on. Our Lean transformation efforts uncovered more opportunities resulting in more improvements than I can share. The multitude of projects in which our leaders and team members engaged was nothing short of heroic. We still had to take care of the day-to-day business of caring for our patients, which made it especially challenging to spend so much time in improvement efforts. Consequently, as anticipated, our jobs got harder before they got easier.

Well, in a way. We certainly had to work longer and harder. But in a way our jobs also got immediately easier. We had a vision of what we wanted to achieve. We had seen success in our initial rev cycle and ED projects, and we were confident that we could successfully transform Healing U. In some ways, it was a very fun time. As overwhelmed as we all were, the camaraderie, the pulling together as a team to accomplish our shared vision, the mutual commitment that we all shared—these, coupled with the hope and belief that we could achieve a better Healing U—was an inspiration to us all. Our nurses and the rest of our staff got excited and engaged in the transformation, and decided to stick around to help make it happen. Turnover declined sharply. The successes along the way kept the 'motivational flywheel' turning. It truly was a labor of love. As gold is refined in fire, so our team was honed by the transformation experience. And we all took immense pride in our accomplishments.

After less than three short years—that at times seemed like an eternity—the many "smaller" wins rolled up into some major organizational improvements: patient care and safety, patient and team member satisfaction, and bottom line results. We are now in the 80th plus percentile range on patient sat. Discharge instructions are reliably provided 100% of the time. Physician complaints are fewer and farther between. In fact, many of the docs that do cases with our competitor are increasingly hearing about the good things going on at Healing U, and I meet with them on a much more frequent basis about joining our team. Our market share has improved. And we now generate the margins we need to reinvest into the system and the community.

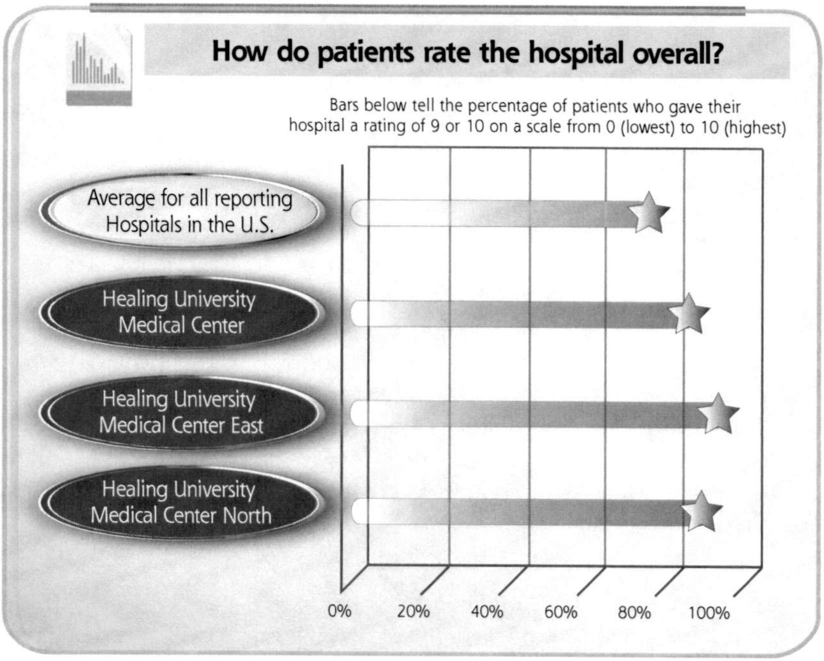

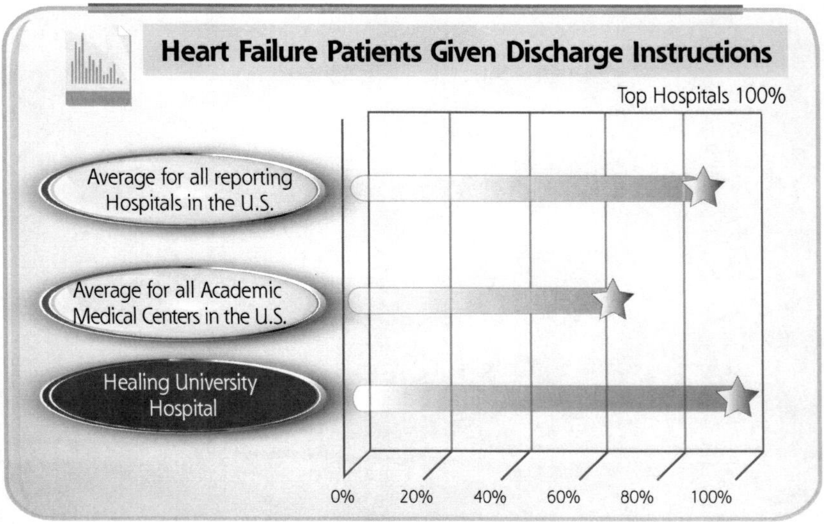
Heart Failure Patients Given Discharge Instructions
Top Hospitals 100%
Average for all reporting Hospitals in the U.S.
Average for all Academic Medical Centers in the U.S.
Healing University Hospital
0%
20%
40%
60%
80%
100%

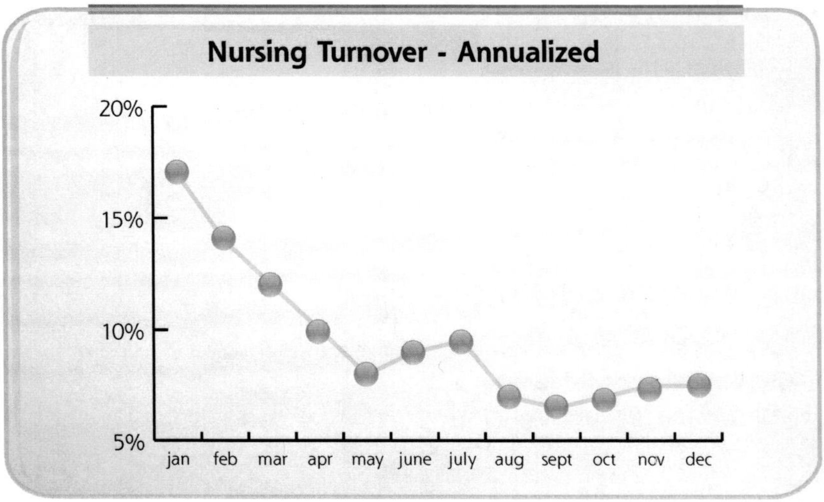
Nursing Turnover - Annualized
20%
15%
10%
5%
jan
feb
mar
apr
may
june
july
aug
sept
oct
nov
dec

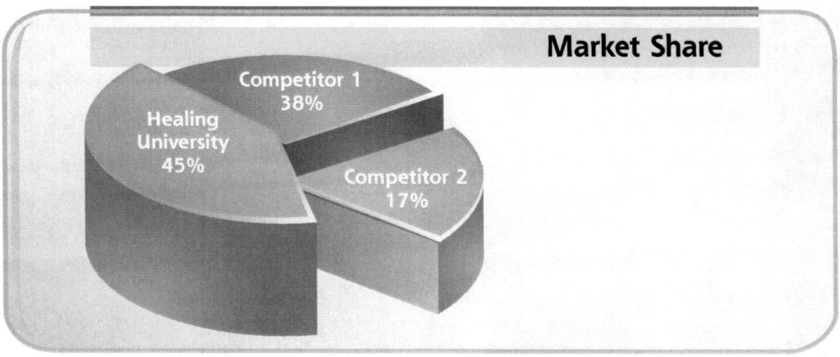
Market Share
Competitor 1 38%
Healing University 45%
Competitor 2 17%

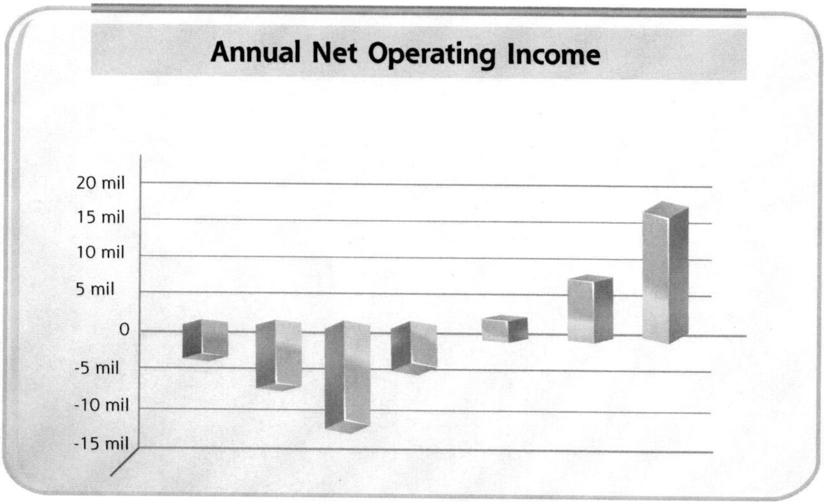

Most importantly, we are all now very proud of the care we deliver, and recommend Healing U without reservation. Whether family, friend, or complete stranger, we are confident that we provide as good care as is available. That is what I am most proud of.

One recent night at dinner, I got a call from our neighbor, Gary. He was the guy who had such a horrible experience with Healing U's ER when he had appendicitis. Gary called to tell me that despite his bad experience a few years ago, he was giving Healing U another chance. Gary is slated to have a knee replacement at Healing U next week. In talking with me and by word-of-mouth from other friends Gary decided that we really had made a turnaround. He told me he was very impressed with articles about Healing U in the newspaper. He had a consult with an orthopedic surgeon who does surgeries at Healing U and at our competitor's hospital. The physician had actually recommended Healing U to Gary because he prefers to do surgeries there due to their timeliness and excellent patient care. What an endorsement!

It was a proud moment for me to know that my neighbor was willing to give my hospital a second chance. I felt very confident that his experience would be the exact opposite of last time. It pleased me, too, that a surgeon also preferred to do treatments at our hospital. If one physician feels that way, it's quite likely that others do too.

Chapter TWENTY

Reflections on the Journey

Occasionally I look back and review our journey to date. Yes, I actually have time these days for contemplation! Now I can actually breathe, relax, and consider where we have come, and more importantly where we are going and how we are going to get there. That can happen when you no longer have to spend all your time freeing up beds so you can go off of diversion, listening to righteously indignant physicians complain about broken OR processes, or just in general fight the myriad fires we are accustomed to in this industry.

Although we will never stop striving and working to achieve Perfect Care, a tremendous amount of our work is complete. That doesn't mean I don't have to stay late at work every now and then, but my schedule is definitely becoming more predictable. Amy and Tyler seem to be happy about the amount of time I'm able to spend at home and we're even planning a family vacation.

From time to time I continue to review my notes from the transformation. Whenever I do, something sticks out at me. Sometimes something new; sometimes a reinforcement of a prior insight. As I read it again this moment, it is the need for a stable system that seems most striking. Healthcare delivery is so very complex. We need to be able to reliably and consistently provide our care in the way designed. Standardizing our processes, documenting where valuable, and consistently following them is the foundational key to managing this complexity. Doing that alone would radically reduce, if not eliminate, patient harm.

Then, once a culture of compliance stabilizes the system, the work of continual improvement can begin. Our improvement efforts can then bear great fruit. Once we have learned how to standardize, only then can we begin the work of identifying and standardizing best practices. And when we master that, we can truly thrive.

We do it all through people: our team members, our managers and leaders, our teachers, and yes our consultants. As the senior leaders, we have a responsibility to learn and grow, so that we may better lead our organization and free our people to do the jobs we hired them to do. We take these lessons from our teachers and consultants. We read books. We think. We learn.

But then we must act. Executives cannot just support an initiative. They have to be active leaders and participants. I often recall the lesson I learned on the revenue cycle project, when after the initial energy and excitement faded it began to bog down. When Paul found out I had not been as active as he thought an executive sponsor should be, he let me know about it in no uncertain terms. His sternness and the not-so-friendly conversation that ensued seemed a bit of an overreaction to me at the time. But not to Paul; he wouldn't let it go. He wouldn't let me off the hook until I repeated it back to him and promised to do it: "I have to maintain focus—a rallying cry if you will—provide support, and eliminate barriers to successful execution. I can best do that by staying involved in regularly scheduled out-briefs with the team."

As usual, Paul couldn't have been more right. I have since paid attention to that mild rebuke, not just within Healing U, but also in other organizations. Without fail, initiatives led by the senior executive succeed where others fail. We, the senior leaders must ensure that the organization continues to value the importance of the effort. We must ensure a steady drumbeat of progress in response to continued follow-up, focus and accountability. This is not a role that we can successfully delegate to consultants or senior staff. We have to do it. This is perhaps the most important lesson I have learned: *when engaged in organizational transformation, the probability of success is directly proportional to the senior executive's commitment and level of personal involvement*.

We must use the knowledge we have gained to remove the bonds that bind our people to the status quo, to rework, to frustration, to poor patient care. Not only do they not resist, I learned that when we include them in the improvement event, they go so far as to thank us for letting them participate!

What a powerful lesson! And so true; we have willing workers. They want to do a good job. We, management, own the system in which they work. It is our responsibility to make it better, to eliminate barriers so they can do their jobs. Improving the system is often just as simple as asking our people what the barriers are, drawing on their expertise, trusting their advice, and making the improvements that they already know are so badly needed. Once we learned that great lesson, our Lean journey became a very inspiring and empowering process for the leadership team and for all our team members, and there was no shortage of ideas or enthusiasm for driving process improvement.

There was a time when I would have thought that we "had arrived!" But now I realize we will never "arrive." I have learned a lot along the way. Our people have grown in knowledge, understanding, and commitment. Healing University has improved its care of patients, its physician and team member satisfaction, and its operational performance. And yes, we have reached some points along the way that we may have once considered destinations.

But we're not yet "there," and never will be. We are certainly a lot closer than we were when we began. Our turnaround has been no less than phenomenal. It exceeded my every expectation. As Paul encouraged, this journey of a thousand miles did begin with one step. That was many steps ago. And yet, I know there are many still before us. Empowering our people to standardize best practices is the path of least resistance.

The old saying is true: the more you know, the more you know you don't know. Or in this case, the more we have accomplished, the more we know there is to accomplish. Our Destination is Perfect Care. We will never get there. But we will keep improving. We will get closer and closer. Our possibilities are endless. I am excited to provide care to those in need. And I look excitedly at what the future holds for those of us with the vision, the passion, and the will to create a better tomorrow.

How about you?

Epilogue

I'm in a meeting with the newly installed CEO from Bethany Memorial Healthcare system. She's dealing with a lot of the same issues I was just a few short years ago—internal challenges like OR turnover, inpatient throughput, ED holds, nursing turnover, physician dissatisfaction, CMS audits, etc., etc.; and external challenges like increased competition, increased regulation, decreased reimbursement, and higher self-pay. She's a bit overwhelmed, as I was. I remember sitting in her chair in my first meeting with Paul. Wow—I couldn't have imagined I'd be in his chair at some point, but here I am. What a nice feeling!

We just finished the tour and are back in my office. I see a slight glimmer of hope in her eyes—a glimmer I am familiar with. She is clearly excited and scared at the same time. She finally gets to the question:

"So what is your secret?" she asks.

I give a little pause, and say "It's quite simple really. It's about the people. And it's about the process. We empower our people to improve our processes."

But you know the rest of the story. And if I can do it, you can do it.

Go do it!

About the Author

Mark L. Dean PhD

Dr. Mark Dean is an innovative thought leader and seasoned executive with over 30 years' experience in healthcare, government, academia, and industry. He holds a doctorate degree in clinical psychology and master's degrees in electrical engineering and management. Dr. Dean has successfully guided health care, engineering, manufacturing and service organizations in their pursuits of organizational excellence by facilitating the development and implementation of leadership systems that integrate strategic, operational and quality improvement initiatives.

Before returning to consulting, Dr. Dean most recently served as the Senior Executive for Performance Improvement with **Jewish Hospital & St. Mary's Healthcare**. There he developed and refined his approach for organizational transformation, and helped lead a successful turnaround initiative. In his consulting practice, he provides executive coaching and leadership development, team building, and strategic guidance and support for organizational transformation initiatives.

Dr. Dean has served as a professor of Organizational Leadership at **Purdue University**, where he taught courses on leadership, human behavior in organizations, and process improvement. He has numerous publications in the areas of Leadership, Quality Improvement, and the Social Systems model. These include serving as the Keynote Speaker at the **11th Annual Deming Research Seminar**, and an article entitled "*Does Baldrige Make its Business Case*" in the **American Society for Quality's (ASQ)** flagship publication *Quality Progress*.

Dr. Dean is a Licensed Clinical Psychologist, and an American Society for Quality Certified Quality Engineer and Six Sigma Black Belt. He has a wonderful family with four grown children and two grandchildren.

To engage in a dialogue or provide feedback, the author may be reached at MarkLDean@aol.com

Glossary & Acronyms

5S (Sort, Set in Order, Shine, Standardize, Sustain) – A 5S is an improvement activity focused on cleaning up and maintaining the order of a work space. The intent is to decrease waste, increase flow and improve quality and productivity by minimizing errors.

Affinity Diagram – a business tool used to organize ideas and data.

ALOS – Average Length of Stay. The duration of a patient's stay in either an inpatient unit or the ER.

Circle Diagram – a diagram similar to a spaghetti diagram used to identify unnecessary processing. Ideal for mapping flow of information and communication.

CMO – Chief Medical Officer

CNO – Chief Nursing Officer

Continuous Flow – the sequencing of activities through the service process one task "unit of work" at a time to minimize delays and reduce the overall lead time.

Corrective and Preventive Action Program – an active organizational program for following up on corrective and preventive actions identified through the internal process audit and any other methods of identifying noncompliance to operational policies and procedures.

Demand – the desire of purchasers, consumers, etc. for a particular commodity or service.

Deployment – refers to the depth and breadth of the enterprise transformation across the organization, and is a measure of the maturity of the initiative.

ED – Emergency Department

Enterprise Map – a high level diagram of the internal service delivery activities of an organization. Typically each of these activities comprises a Value Stream/Healing Pathway.

Flow – an ideal process state in which patients, products or materials move smoothly through the process with no delays or bottlenecks.

Healing Pathway – a value stream through which patients flow. An example is the treatment of a patient in the Emergency Department.

Healing Pathway Analysis (HPA) – a structured and facilitated event during which a cross-functional team progresses methodically through a series of interactive and evaluative steps aimed at eliminating impediments to healing and improving the flow of patients through the healing pathway.

Just Do It (JDI) – an action for which no additional study or decision making is necessary. All information and knowledge necessary to decide on the process change is available, and the team readily and easily agrees. The team has decided it should be done, and all that is left is for someone to make it happen.

Internal Process Audit Program – a systematic, documented, and ongoing review of organizational compliance to policies and procedures, including meeting the training and certification needs of all members.

Kanban System – a method of using cards or other signaling devices as visual signals for triggering or controlling the flow of materials and supplies.

Lean – a continual improvement methodology that focuses on improving value by eliminating waste and increasing throughput in customer driven value streams.

Lean Sigma – a process improvement approach that combines Lean's focus on the elimination of waste and improvement in throughput with Six Sigma's focus on reducing variability and eliminating defects.

LWBS – Left Without Being Seen. A measure of the percentage of patients who show up at the emergency room and leave before being seen, usually due to delay in receiving care.

LOS – Length of Stay.

Non Value Added Activity – Activities performed during the production or delivery of a product or service that utilize time or resources, but do not increase its value to the customer. There are two types of Non Value Added Activities. The first type are those activities that are "non-value added but required," due to regulatory, legal, or other requirements. The second type are those activities that are "non-value added" and not required. This second type is also called "Waste."

PDCA Cycle – Plan, Do, Check, Act. A model that represents a continual improvement cycle.

Process – a set of steps that transform one or more inputs into one or more outputs.

Project – A Project is an improvement activity that entails analysis, is typically data analytic, and is often conducted by an engineer or team to determine the best approach for achieving a desired outcome.

Pull System – A delivery system in which goods are produced or services provided only when requested by a downstream process. A customer's order "pulls" a product or service from the delivery system. Nothing is produced until it is needed or wanted downstream. Compare to push system.

Push System - A delivery system in which goods are produced or services provided and handed off to a downstream process, where they are stored until needed. This type of system creates excess inventory. Compare to pull system.

Quality Management System – A comprehensive, integrated, and interdependent set of policies, procedures, checklists; enabled by employee training, development, and certification; maintained by a culture of compliance including an internal process audit program, corrective action system, and personal and organizational accountability; that leads to the reliable and repeatable provision of products and services.

Queue – a line or sequence of people, equipment, tasks, and so on awaiting their turn to be attended to or to proceed.

Queuing Strategies – queuing (sequencing) techniques used to analyze and subsequently match service resources in terms of capability, capacity, and timing to demand requirements of the customer.

Quick Changeover – A method of analyzing an organization's processes and then reducing the materials, skilled resources, and time needed for equipment setup. It allows an organization to implement small-batch production or one-piece flow in a cost-effective manner. Also called set up reduction.

Rapid Improvement Event (RIE) aka Kaizen – a facilitated, structured, team-based event aimed at further refining and actually implementing improvements to portions of a value stream.

Rapid Improvement Newspaper – a tracking tool used to ensure completion of actions identified during an RIE that cannot be completed during the actual event.

Rapid Improvement Plan – a plan for transforming the current state of a value stream or healing pathway to the desired future state. A rapid improvement plan will typically identify multiple "Just-Do-Its," "Rapid Improvement Events," and "Projects." It will also identify who is responsible for leading each effort, and a date by when it will be completed.

Return on Investment (ROI) – Profit from an investment as a percentage of the amount invested.

Root Cause Analysis – A process for identifying problems, finding their causes, and creating the best solutions to keep them from happening again.

SIPOC (Supplier Input Process Output Customer) Diagram – a tool used to identify all relevant elements of a process improvement effort.

Six Sigma – a statistical concept that refers to the amount of variation in a process. In addition to being a statistical measure of variation the term also refers to a continual improvement methodology aimed at reducing defects.

Spaghetti Diagram – a very useful graphic that shows how people or things flow in a physical layout.

Standard Operating Procedures (SOPs) – Reliable instructions that describe the correct and most effective way to get a work process done.

Standard Operations – The most efficient work combination that an organization can put together.

Statistical Process Control (SPC) – The use of mathematics and statistical measurements to solve an organization's problems and build quality into its products and services.

Statistical Control – Measure of stability in a system. Lack of control can be caused by inconsistent adherence to policies and procedures, creating process variation that reverberates through the system, creating delays, dissatisfaction and inefficiency.

Supply – make products or services available to satisfy a requirement or demand.

Takt Time – The total available work time per day (or shift) divided by customer-demand requirements per day (or shift). Takt time sets the pace of production to match the rate of customer demand. For example, if your customers demand 480 x-rays per day and your radiology department line operates 960 minutes per day, takt time is two minutes.

Theory of Constraints – a concept, introduced by Eliyahu Goldratt in the novel The Goal, which focuses on the removal of impediments (constraints) to process flow.

Total Costs – is the sum total of purchase price, acquisition, possession and disposal costs. Also known as total cost of ownership (TCO) and lifecycle costs of a product or service.

Transformation Summit – a planning offsite during which the CEO and Senior Leadership Team plan the Enterprise Transformation.

Transformation Team – a team under the leadership of an executive sponsor, charged to transform a value stream or healing pathway.

Value Added Activity – Activity performed during the production or delivery of a product or service that increase its value to the customer.

Value Stream – a set of one or more processes that result in the delivery of a product or service.

Value Stream Analysis (VSA) – a structured and facilitated event during which a cross-functional team progresses methodically through a series of interactive and evaluative steps aimed at increasing value by eliminating waste and improving the flow of products or services through the value stream.

Value Stream Map – An illustration that uses simple graphics or icons to show the sequence and movement of information, materials, and actions in a company's value stream.

Waste – any type of activity performed during the production or delivery of a service or product that utilizes time or resources, but does not increase value to the customer; and that is not required for legal, regulatory, or other reasons.